PLANNING FOR
EDUCATIONAL REFORM
Financial and
Social Alternatives

LINDLEY J. STILES
Professor of Education for Interdisciplinary Studies
Northwestern University
Advisory Editor to Dodd, Mead & Company

PLANNING FOR EDUCATIONAL REFORM

Financial and

Social Alternatives

by
CHARLES S. BENSON
PAUL M. GOLDFINGER
E. GARETH HOACHLANDER
JESSICA S. PERS

DODD, MEAD & COMPANY
New York   1974

EDITOR'S INTRODUCTION

Refinancing elementary and secondary education is a first priority in the United States today. Traditional ways of raising and distributing school revenues are no lo..ger acceptable or legally defensible—either educationally or in terms of taxation policy. They fail to assure equal educational opportunities for students and place disparate financial burdens on cities and communities.

Efforts by states to equalize school costs and per-pupil support with supplemental grants to poorer school districts have not been too successful. Appraised property values differ so much from district to district that it is almost impossible to establish and maintain fair ability and effort formulas. Also, with some statewide revenue plans, such as the sales tax, the lower-income districts may actually provide a greater share of the equalizing funds. Then, too, in the politics of state finance the richer districts are able to generate greater pressures; as a consequence, when increases in state aid for schools are made, they tend to be in the form of flat grants without reference to local resources and effort. The pattern that results, as the authors of this extraordinary book point out, is one in which the difference in per-pupil support may range from a low of $197 to a high of $11,096 from one district to another and within the same state. Although this is an extreme example, the normal ranges of differences in per-pupil expenditures are great enough to remind us the quality of education a student receives, as judged by the price at least, depends for the most part on where he or she lives.

Complicating theories and practices of educational finance even more is the fact that equal support does not produce equality in learning. So many factors bear upon how well any individual student will take advantage of educational opportunities that it is almost impossible to prove that equalizing school expenditures will make a difference, particularly for those who need help most. We know that the quality of education a school provides is not always related on a one-to-one ratio to per-pupil costs. Some school districts with modest means—because of such factors as geographical location, community attitudes, philosophy of education, leadership, or personnel policies—are able to attract and retain good teachers and administrators. The curriculum, instructional resources and strategies, as well as disciplinary standards of a school all contribute to educational productivity. The kind of students enrolled is a crucial factor. Similarly, stability of family and community life as well as other conditions that motivate interest in learning can make a difference. Underlying all such considerations is the persistent but as yet unanswered question: Should not the goal be to promote equality in achievement—at defined maximum levels at least—rather than equal per-pupil expenditures?

The questions about school finance come easily, of course; workable answers are more difficult to generate. Herein lies the significant contributions of this timely book. The authors not only identify the issues, they propose solutions that will make dollars invested in our schools make sense. The outcomes they judge to be worth the investment are seen as beneficial to the society as a whole as well as to the individual student. The changes they propose grow out of the best that is known and provide adequate safeguards against the pressures of special interests and the wide variations in family and community attitudes. In short, this is a book that brings practical help to educators and others interested in refinancing and reforming our elementary and secondary schools.

Dr. Charles S. Benson, senior author of this book, is a leading authority on school finance in the United States. His assessments of current problems and proposed solutions are sought and respected by educational and political leaders as well as by school board members and others who wrestle with finding ways to support our schools. Each of Dr. Benson's co-authors, Paul M. Goldfinger, E. Gareth Hoachlander, and Jessica S. Pers, brought to the writing qualities of scholarship and experience that made for a broad look at the educational reforms needed in the years ahead. Together, this interdisciplinary team of scholars has carefully analyzed the existing state of American educational enterprise and proposed reforms that make extraordinarily good sense. I predict that this book will become a *landmark* volume, a guide for refinancing our schools, and a spotlight on needed educational reforms.

LINDLEY J. STILES

PREFACE

This volume on reform of our system of public education has developed from our shared experience in working on major policy studies in two large states: New York and California. In New York we were staff members (except Gary Hoachlander) of the Fleischmann Commission (1970–72) and in California we served as consultants (except Jessica Pers) to the Senate Select Committee on School District Finance (1971–72). Our work in education is not confined, of course, to these two assignments, but they are of special importance for us because during these particular periods of activity, the work of reform-minded state legislators and policy analysts was reinforced by the judiciary, as, for example, in the *Serrano* case in California.

Necessarily, indeed desirably, work for public commissions and state legislatures is bounded by constraints of time and political pressures. This volume is a reflective one in which we explore, insofar as we are able, the deeper issues of reform of the system of financing schools. In it we also speculate on what directions structural revision of education might take. We are wholly convinced that the issues we try to illuminate are among the most strategic in shaping a new America, for they affect intimately the degree to which we shall achieve social class integration, revitalization of metropolitan life, and proper exercise of household choice in the public sector. We hope the reader agrees that the questions we raise are significant, though he or she need not agree with our conclusions.

Our debts are many, especially to our fellow workers on the Fleischmann Commission and the California study. Likewise, we owe much to our friends in state legislatures, those "secular saints," who would probably prefer to be unnamed. Among academics, we express particular gratitude to Professors Henry M. Levin, Stanford, and John E. Coons, Berkeley. Both are on record as taking issue with some of our conclusions, but since the matters discussed here are contentious, full agreement is not to be expected. We hope, simply, to contribute to a more thorough discussion of the matters at hand.

The typescript of this book was prepared by Mary B. Norton and Norma Levingston.

All of the authors of this book are presently associated with the Childhood and Government Project, School of Law (Boalt Hall), University of California, Berkeley, California. This project is funded by the Ford Foundation and Carnegie Corporation. We gratefully acknowledge the financial assistance of these foundations but we absolve them wholly of the responsibility for our arguments and proposals.

CHARLES S. BENSON
PAUL M. GOLDFINGER
E. GARETH HOACHLANDER
JESSICA S. PERS

CONTENTS

1

INTRODUCTION

In 1899 in the first lectures that form *The School and Society,* John Dewey said: "What the best and wisest parent wants for his own child, that must the community want for all its children. Any other idea for our schools is narrow and unlovely; acted upon, it destroys our democracy." Few would disagree with Dewey. Most Americans view education as the primary means for providing young people with the skills, abilities, and insights essential for living and growing in an increasingly complicated world, and they want only the best education available.

But if American schools are viewed in the light of Dewey's statement, we can only conclude that they are indeed "narrow and unlovely." Supreme Court Justice Potter Stewart recently described our system of public education as "chaotic and unjust." Some American schools offer students stimulating atmospheres with modern, spacious buildings, skilled staffs, and numerous services. Others though, especially many urban schools, are in shambles; deteriorating buildings are pockmarked with broken windows, staffed by inexperienced teachers, and crowded with bored, alienated students. Rural schools often lack adequate facilities for instruction in basic science, foreign languages, art, and music, and their geographic isolation often excludes students from the multicultured diversity of metropolitan areas. Some suburban schools cannot afford to attract highly trained staffs to offer advanced mathematics, biology, career counseling, and other special services. Perhaps these less fortunate communities have not yet found, in Dewey's words, the "best and wisest parent" among them as a guide; more likely, they know what they want but are unable to obtain it.

The system for allocating educational resources—one of our basic concerns here—works to the advantage of some and disadvantage of others. Glaring financial inequities in educational provision have disturbed reformers and social critics throughout recent decades; they disturb us also. But other inequities seem more glaring and pernicious—the existence of racial and social isolation in the schools and the unavailability of educational alternatives within the public sector. In large measure we will discuss these aspects in relation to the poor; but our basic concern is for *all* children who are the consumers of public education.

Primarily, this book promotes equity in public education, that is, standards of fairness and impartiality for schools that operate in a society of increasingly diverse interests and values. The authors share a definite viewpoint: we believe that the public schools should not reflect the gross disparities of income and wealth that exist in our society. This belief leads us to favor, among other reforms, income redistribution. Moreover, we stress the importance of racial and social integration, not because we seek the bland homogeneity of a melting pot but because we value the stimulation and growth afforded by interaction among different individuals. Finally, we believe that the educational system must offer more varied programs, services, and methodologies to students and their parents. Ideally, students should be allowed to choose educational services appropriate to individual interests and learning requirements.

Equity in public education—our larger concern—is not the same as equality. More often than not, we will be promoting educational inequality. Equity and inequality are not necessarily opposites. In fact, promoting equity may *require* inequality, as shown by Will Riggan:

We have been so caught up, entangled, in this tub-thumping phrase or in reaction against its operational weaknesses that to *promote inequality* is, at first blush, heresy. But it is heresy at first blush only, for what I am suggesting is that our constituents and our personal sanity may both be better served by approaching the problems of improving lower education in our respective states by careful consideration of which inequalities we wish to promote and which abolish.

The nation's schools do not now treat all children equally, nor for some purposes should they. While there is a proper hue and cry over gross expenditure inequalities that are the result of unequal taxable wealth in various communities, there are at the same time few who begrudge spending more money on the education of a physically handicapped child than on a so-called normal student. In point of fact, our education systems are, in the ways they treat taxpayers and students, constantly creating or reproducing inequalities.

However, deciding today which inequalities are beneficial and which are pernicious and then acting accordingly goes far beyond equalizing tax burdens and expenditures within a state, though that kind of redress is virtually a prerequisite.[1]

We do not promote equity of educational provision as a goal for its own sake. Different people with different interests and outlooks should, of course, expect different outcomes from their educational experiences. Schools touch almost everyone—from practically every social stratum and background. Thus, they influence individuals without regard to where they come from or where they are likely to end up. The schools then must promote equity, especially because other institutions seem to function without any regard for it. Education cannot, of course, cure all social ills. But, at the very least, greater equity in educational expenditures and provision can foster greater equity in both educational consumption and in the ultimate welfare of educated persons. The Robbins Committee, an education committee in England, has noted that "education ministers intimately to ultimate ends, in developing man's capacity to understand, to contemplate, and to create. And it is a characteristic of the aspirations of this age to feel that, where there is capacity to pursue such activities, then that capacity should be fostered. The good society desires equality of opportunity for its citizens to become not merely good producers but also good men and women."[2]

A Brief Look at the Present System

Attention to some facts and figures will help convey a sense of the magnitude of American education and the inequities produced by the present system.

During the 1972–73 school year, local, state, and federal governments spent a total of $51.9 billion on elementary and secondary education. Had this amount been distributed equally, it would have provided $1,133 for educating each of the nation's 45.8 million public school students. In addition to being one of the largest industries in the nation, public education

[1] Will Riggan, "School Finance Research in the Seventies," A Paper Prepared for a Conference of the National Education Finance Project (Atlanta, Ga., April 3, 1973), pp. 3–4.

[2] The Robbins Committee on Higher Education, *Higher Education* (London: Her Majesty's Stationery Office, 1963), p. 8.

has also been one of the fastest growing. During the 1960s, expenditures on elementary and secondary education increased at an annual rate of 10 percent, reflecting rising enrollments, inflation, and increased demand for educational services. But American public education cannot accurately be described as a single, unified industry. It is the most decentralized educational system in the world. Each school district—over 15,000 in the fifty states—possesses some degree of autonomy and responsibility for financing and administering public education. Decentralization produces wide variations in expenditures, facilities, personnel, curriculum, and methodology.

In our federal system each level of government, local, state, and federal, assumes some responsibility for financing education. The federal government's role has traditionally been minimal, with Washington contributing about 7 percent of revenues in 1971–72. With the exception of Hawaii, where state revenues provide virtually all of the funds for education, the *basic mechanics* of state funding are similar from state to state.

In distributing aid for education state governments try to equalize financial resources among local school districts. The mechanics of distribution are complex and appear to promote equalization; in truth, however, the state schemes fail to counter existing financial disparities among districts. State finance schemes are described in the Appendix at the end of this chapter.

The range of specified minimums in "equalization formulas" the size of "basic grants," and procedures for allocating "categorical aid" (see Appendix to this chapter for a thorough discussion of these terms) differ greatly among the states. Thus in 1971–72, local revenues (primarily local property taxes) represented an average of 54 percent of total revenues used for public elementary and secondary education. State sources supplied 39 percent of the revenues. These averages are deceptive, however. In Hawaii, where the state funds education, local revenues in the same period represented less than 2 percent of total receipts. At the other end of the spectrum local governments in New Hampshire were responsible for raising over 85 percent of total receipts. In 1971–72 local governments contributed more than 60 percent of revenues in nineteen states and less than 35 percent in twelve others. Variations within states are often equally dramatic. In California, for example, the average local contribution for all districts was 58 percent. But some districts contributed less than 15 percent, while others, like the oil-rich McKittrick Elementary District, contributed over 90 percent. Federal support also varied widely, ranging from a minimum of 2.3 percent in Connecticut to a maximum 28.1 percent in Mississippi.

Can these differences in revenue sources be explained as attempts to rationalize per-student spending among states and local districts? Are the measures to allow districts the opportunity to obtain an appropriate amount of resources for instruction of students? Unfortunately, this is not the case. In 1972–73 statewide average expenditures per student ranged from a low of $590 in Alabama to a high of $1,584 in New York. Within states the divergence was even more pronounced. In California district per-pupil expenditures ranged from $402 to $3,187; in Massachusetts from $454 to $4,243; in Georgia, from $364 to $735; and in Texas from $197 to $11,096. Even if the highest spending 10 percent of all districts in each state is excluded from comparison, the remaining high-spending districts in most states still spend more than twice as much as the low spenders, as in Alaska, where the amounts varied from $1,254 to $480.

The figures suggest large disparities in the quality and cost of education available from state to state and within each as well. We must proceed with caution, however. First, the figures do not reflect cost-of-living differences within or among states. While the costs of such items as textbooks, audio-visual equipment, school furnishings, and classroom supplies vary little from region to region, these items make up a surprisingly small fraction of a school's budget. Sixty-five to 80 percent of the budget in most school districts is allocated to salaries of teachers, administrators, and clerical and maintenance personnel. Thus, the difference in expenditure levels between New York and Alabama can be explained by the fact that it costs much more for a person to live in New York than in Alabama. Second, unusually high expenditures, such as $11,096 per student in one Texas district, frequently reflect the costs of education in rural districts having especially small student populations. Third, high expenditures in very wealthy districts often support items that many believe do not contribute directly to the purposes of public education—olympic-sized swimming pools, elaborate lighting systems for stage productions, wall-to-wall carpeting, and so on. Fourth, higher expenditures in central cities are explained somewhat by larger outlays for security, insurance, and maintenance of old buildings. These expenditures do not raise the quality of education in cities, but they are necessary to keep the schools running.

Dollars per se, then, are not education. They simply purchase a mix of educational inputs; equal dollar amounts can purchase very different mixes of teachers, counselors, administrators, textbooks, libraries, school buildings, and teaching equipment. Districts that spend equal amounts of money on each pupil may spend it in different ways. Whereas one may hire fewer teachers and more counselors, another may hire fewer teachers and counselors but operate a closed-circuit television system. Still another may devote money to more attractive or larger physical facilities. Whether these different educational inputs support programs of similar educational quality depends upon whether they obtain similar results.

Dollars and Educational Outputs

But to determine the relationship between inputs and final results and obtain maximum educational quality from dollars spent, measurement is essential. In education knowledge of this input-output relationship (or production function) is primitive.

This leads us into the important and perplexing problem of defining and measuring the results of education. The traditional measuring instruments are tests of student achievement. Educators and educational critics rarely agree, however, on what achievement tests really measure. Such tests tell us little about a student's enjoyment of learning, whether he has gained a deeper awareness of himself and a better understanding of social and cultural values, or whether he will become a thoughtful, capable adult. More cynically, some feel that these tests measure little more than a student's achievement in taking tests, perhaps not a trivial achievement in a competitive, test-oriented society. But if the purpose of education is merely to improve students' mastery of taking tests, then the "results" of education are narrow and mediocre at best.

Our schools do not rely on testing because they are solely concerned with equipping students with a few basic skills. Rather, these few basic skills—reading, mathematics, and fact regurgitation—are the only educational products that tests currently measure. Moreover, many are uncomfortably suspicious that tests do not even measure these very well. Even if examination is restricted to analyzing the effects of different inputs on achievement test scores, the results are often contradictory and uncertain. Some studies maintain that variations in class size, a teacher's race, experience, and academic achievement, the time spent in guidance activities, absenteeism, and science laboratory facilities are significantly related to changes in pupil achievement.[3] Other analysts claim that variations in a

[3] Eric A. Hanushek, "The Education of Negroes and Whites" (Ph.D. diss., Massachusetts Institute of Technology, 1968); Samuel Bowles, "Towards an Educational Produc-

student's family background and native intelligence account for most of the differences in achievement and that variations in school curricula, facilities, and staff have only a very small effect.[4]

Do dollars make a difference in education? On the basis of existing research this question cannot be answered unequivocably. The input-output relationships in education are remarkably complex, and today's research procedures are not sophisticated enough to untangle them. Logically, there must be some point at which the returns from additional spending are not worth the cost. Nevertheless, existing research is presently unable to determine what this level of expenditure should be.

Although a correct spending level cannot yet be established, the input-output problem raises another more immediate question. Precisely what is meant by "equal opportunity" in education, equal inputs or outputs? Input equality requires that the same amount of economic resources be spent on all students. Because the price of educational resources may differ from place to place, equal dollar expenditures do not necessarily yield the true result of input equality. In addition, even if districts reported equal *real* expenditures per student, not all students in the districts may be receiving equal treatment, for some schools within districts may be favored and others disadvantaged. So difficult problems stand in the way of achieving input equality, though the idea itself is straightforward. Output equality refers to a condition under which any set of students of equal ability display average standards of school performance that are equal. In this case, also, there are difficulties in determining equality of treatment and equality of school performance.

Most people would probably argue for equal inputs of dollars, because more sophisticated schemes for establishing "equal opportunity" in education might seem impossible to implement.

Though little is known about the effects of equalizing financial inputs to every student, it is worth looking briefly at the experience in Hawaii. Hawaii is the only state without independent school districts. Statewide income and sales taxes finance Hawaiian schools, and funds are allocated at

---

tion Function," in W. Lee Hansen, ed., *Education, Income and Human Capital* (New York: National Bureau of Economic Research, 1970), pp. 11–60; Eric A. Hanushek, "Teacher Characteristics and Gains in Student Achievement: Estimation Using Micro Data," *American Economic Review*, 61 (May 1971): 280–88; Henry M. Levin, "A New Model of School Effectiveness," *Do Teachers Make a Difference?*, U.S. Department of Health, Education, and Welfare (Washington, D.C.: Government Printing Office, 1970), pp. 55–78.

[4] James S. Coleman et al., *Equality of Educational Opportunity* (Washington, D.C.: Government Printing Office, 1966); Christopher Jencks et al., *Inequality: A Reassessment of the Effect of Family and Schooling in America* (New York: Basic Books, Inc., 1972).

$930 per pupil. School buildings are of similar quality, and the pupil-teacher ratio, 26 to 1, is about the same in every school. Nevertheless, results on educational achievement tests in Hawaii show the same discrepancies from district to district as in other states. Honolulu's Kahala Elementary School and Palolo Elementary School, for example, have similar physical facilities, employ similarly skilled teachers, and use the same curriculum; but children in Kahala consistently score twice as high as Palolo's students on uniform tests. As one might expect, Kahala's students are predominantly white and live in upper middle-class neighborhoods. Palolo is near a public housing project; about 40 percent of its students come from welfare families of Oriental and Polynesian backgrounds in which English is rarely spoken. Similar examples of discrepancy can be found throughout Hawaii.[5]

Obviously, providing equal dollar inputs for unequal students produces unequal results. Equal spending does not make education the "great equalizer of the conditions of men" as Horace Mann suggested in the last century. If education is to facilitate the movement of the poor and disadvantaged into the mainstream of American social and economic life, if it is to afford everyone equal probability of success (however one defines it), then equal facilities, teaching skills, and curriculums are not the answers. Additional resources must be made available to students who enter and pass through the educational system with handicaps such as language barriers for which they are not responsible. We do not know how much more should be spent to make these additional resources available. Regrettably little research has been done on the impact of various resources on solving educational problems. Thus we are not even confident that we know what kinds of resources should be purchased. Because each student is unique, a technique that aids one may be ineffective for another. Past expenditures have often been wasted; they have been made blindly, without close attention to who receives them, what is purchased, and how effective various resources are. All too often compensatory monies do not reach the students for whom they are intended.

If the System Is Bad, Why Has It Lasted?

But if our system of financing public schools is so inadequate, why has it lasted so long? We recognize that education is compulsory from elemen-

[5] *Time* Magazine, 101, no. 24 (June 11, 1973): 60.

tary school through most of secondary school. Private secular schooling of acceptable standard is available only to a small percentage of the population who can afford it. District boundaries virtually determine which public schools a student can attend. Do we want to conclude that state governments for reasons heartless or vile consciously force large segments of our population to use schools that are demonstrably inferior to schools enjoyed by other members of our society? Most analysts of educational administration are less negative about the system and point to several redeeming features.

First, the present system produces revenue rather well. In March 1973, for example, the Illinois Superintendent's Advisory Committee on School Finance submitted its final report. It voted for full state funding, that is, for the takeover of educational finance by the state government. G. Alan Hickrod, the committee chairman and a long-time analyst of governmental arrangements in education, issued a dissent from the majority recommendation:

> At the present time in Illinois, and in most other states, educators tolerate a certain amount of inequity in school expenditures as the price they pay for engaging in a game of "catch up." The rules are widely known but seldom frankly discussed. Essentially, the game proceeds by having the wealthier districts move their expenditure levels upward, and the education community places pressure on state governments to assist the poorer local districts to catch up, within a reasonable distance, of the leaders. . . . I, for one, am not at this point prepared to give up this game though I do wish to change the rules to favor the poorer districts. Full state funding will end forever our little game of "catch up" and place the decisions regarding how well, or how poorly, K-12 [Kindergarten through secondary school] education will be funded entirely at the state level. . . . I submit it is quite possible that having given up our local leverage factor we could find support for K-12 education languishing as the General Assembly is faced with many demands for state money other than for public education.[6]

Second, the present system maintains the allegiance of more affluent households. Because the suburban rich have exclusive rights to high quality public institutions supported by their local taxables, they do not usually choose to send their children to private schools. Suburban school systems are really better described as quasi-public, because some children are to-

[6] G. Alan Hickrod, *Final Report of the Superintendent's Advisory Committee on School Finance* (Springfield, Ill., April 1973), p. 104.

tally barred from the benefits of these suburban systems. Even so, we have managed to avoid a two-class arrangement under which the affluent shun tax-supported institutions while the rest of the population has no alternative but to use them. Thus, if the rich withdrew from public institutions, status distinctions in American education would probably become substantially greater than they now are.

Hopefully, the more affluent will continue to use public schools. It seems that they have expansive ideas about the amount of money that should properly be spent on schools. At the same time, people of above-average wealth usually exert more influence in both state and local councils of government than their simple numbers would warrant. Because they themselves are often graduates of public schools and send their children to such institutions, they are probably more inclined to urge governmental generosity toward public education.

Third, it is argued that the present system preserves values of localism in government. This argument is commonly used by those who wish to maintain the status quo. Perhaps this argument should be viewed with skepticism. It is true that some small communities maintain a sense of neighborliness in the management of school affairs, and local affairs generally. But some communities use their powers of local control to exclude the poor and nonwhites from their school districts. Indeed, probably the most distressing feature of our system of local government finance is the monetary incentive it provides to perpetuate residential exclusion by race and social class. Furthermore, the advantages of local control, whatever they may be, are very unevenly distributed. Suburbanites may have a strong influence on what goes on in their schools while city dwellers have almost no voice. Residents of big cities might prefer to concentrate their influence on the day-to-day operations of the schools with which they are most immediately involved as parents, teachers, paraprofessionals, administrators, and so on. Indeed, parents and students might welcome an opportunity to choose the type of educational services they "consume." Changes such as these do not depend upon whether the city school board has power to levy local taxes, so the question of whether citizens participate in making decisions about education is not necessarily determined by whether or not they have local fiscal control.

Some believe that local control should be preserved because it allows educational innovation in the districts to test ideas about how school programs could be improved. It is not necessarily true that substitution of state revenue sources for local will stop educational innovation in the districts;

the state need not, and should not, tell districts precisely how to spend their money, and if the districts want to use their resources to conduct experimental programs, adoption of a state system of finance need not stand in their way. Even if a particular type of experiment requires substantial extra resources the state could provide the money from an "innovation fund." The claim of a need for local district experimentation may simply be a method for insuring that suburban districts get additional money to spend on their children. In other words, does local control enhance the productivity of the educational system? Or does it simply whet the appetite for yet more expensive programs? If the answer to the last question is yes, then the argument for local control reduces to one already given—revenue generation. Thus, the school system cannot play "catch up" and maintain the interest of the rich and the middle class in supporting tax increases for schools unless the rich and the middle class are generally able to isolate themselves, their children, and their local taxables in suburban districts, far from the claims of the rest of the population.

There is little justification for perpetuating a finance system that seems primarily to protect racial and social class separateness and encourage high public expenditure for education by allowing wealthy families to cloister their children in "preferred schools." Unquestionably, middle-class distaste for the poor is not new in America. John C. Van Dyke wrote about New York City in 1909:

> If there is any virtue in our boasted home rule of municipalities, then a city should be able, by law, to exclude the vagrant and pauper classes. It might not be possible to do this by threat of prosecution . . . but it could be done, perhaps by taxation. . . . But what are the unfortunates without the gates to do? Where are they to go? . . . Fortunately, so long as these people remain without the gates, New York does not have to answer these questions. It can ignore them.[7]

In the long run, the victims of racial and social class isolation are not only the poor.

> Segregated schools and cruelty in American ghettos are. . . . the institutionalized and inescapable morality of American racism, and as such are deadening and destroying the ethical and personal effectiveness of American white children, and doing so much more insidiously than they are destroying the personal and human effectiveness of American black children. . . . We can . . .

---

[7] John C. Van Dyke, *The New New York* (New York: Macmillan Co., 1909), pp. 262, 266, 267.

save our children . . . from the ethical schizophrenia . . . [and] give them a valuable educational lesson in poise, effectiveness, and security in dealing with people who are superficially different . . . and in that way prepare them to deal effectively with the world, whose outstanding characteristic is that it consists of people who are different. Few other nations have this kind of asset. . . . We could make American schools laboratories by which American youngsters look upon differences as assets . . . .[8]

To pursue these goals envisioned by Kenneth Clark, the conventional method of financing schools must be changed. As we shall demonstrate, the methods for changing school finance arrangements are currently available. These methods do not achieve equity by imposing mediocrity on all users of public education. Instead, they attempt to ensure that the opportunity to obtain higher quality educational services is available to all, not only to the middle and upper classes.

Education and Choice

This concern for fiscal equity does not mean that everyone must receive the same services. Dismantling present financial arrangements that perpetuate fiscal inequity and racial and social class segregation is also a first step toward increasing the variety of educational offerings and assuring that people will be allowed to choose the type of education they desire.

Education reformers rarely accept Christopher Jencks's theory: "If you judge schools according to their long-term effects, and if you believe that these effects are substantial, and if you are an egalitarian, you are likely to feel that everyone should get the same kind of schooling, whether they want it or not." [9] On the contrary, effective education reform must provide services appropriate to the interests and learning requirements of students. And we know that these variables differ widely from one individual to the next. Young people differ, for example, in their responses to the environment of a particular school. A school that stimulates one child to learn may have little effect on another, and it may possibly inhibit the learning of a third. One of the functions of an educational system is to help people discover what their aptitudes, interests, and abilities really are; such discovery is enhanced by diversity of educational experience.

[8] Kenneth Clark, *Hearings Before the Select Committee on Equal Educational Opportunity of the United States Senate* (Washington, D.C.: Government Printing Office, 1970), pp. 76–77.
[9] Jencks, *Inequality: A Reassessment,* p. 16.

At present there may be greater diversity of experience within a well-to-do suburban school than within a ghetto school, but there is not a great deal of difference *between* any two schools in a given region. Suppose, for example, a junior-high student says that science really interests him and that he would like to attend a school in which the faculty and students concentrate on science. This student is asking not only for a specific curricular focus but also for a special atmosphere, embracing an incentive structure that rewards intellectual curiosity and dispassionate, rigorous analysis. It is doubtful that such a public school will be easily found. Another student might be interested in music or painting and look for a school that concentrates on one of these fields. Yet another student might prefer to "work with his hands," in technical, constructional, or mechanical fields. Some students prefer a more unfocused curriculum and would continue by their own choice to attend the kind of school they are attending today. The existing educational system does not offer enough diversity among schools either to help people discover what kinds of lives they want to live or to serve differences in the aptitudes and interests of individuals. As A. C. F. Beale has stated, "one of the profoundest of poverty's degradations . . . is unavailability of choice." [10] Increasing the number of educational options available would do much to moderate this degradation.

There is, of course, a danger in allowing households to make choices in the public sector. Public sector services possess "externalities"; in fact this is why they are tax-supported. Thus a person cares how much of the given service is consumed by other people, not just by himself. This "consumption externality" applies to education as it serves to strengthen the productivity and the social cohesion of a nation. The consumption of such social benefits is a bounty we all share in common and in approximately equal measure. If people were left strictly on their own to choose the amounts and types of educational services they should receive, they might fail to use enough of those that provide social benefits. Formal education is society's instrument for ensuring that all citizens undergo a certain amount of mental discipline. If a few people forego formal education, the effects of their action might be too minor to have an impact on the rest of society. Individuals might be tempted to study only what they wish at any time they wish rather than take part in formalized educational experiences during their formative years. But if these same patterns were followed by most

[10] A. C. F. Beale, "Historical Aspects of the Debate on Education," in *Education: A Framework for Choice* (London: The Institute of Economic Affairs, 1967), p. 20.

pcoplc, society, if it could survive, would lose a great deal. It may matter little if one potentially great natural scientist decides instead to play the flute and make candles, but if all great potential were unrealized, then our inventions and technological advances—and indeed our complex society itself—would diminish.

Besides consumption externalities in education, there are production externalities. How much is learned by a given student is regulated in some degree by the characteristics of his fellow students. It makes a difference, apparently, with whom one goes to school, a difference in how one acquires cognitive skills and, perhaps more important, social sensitivity.

Schools Are Not the Only Means of Social Reform

Schools, obviously, play a crucial role in socializing young people; if nothing else, they physically contain young people for about six hours each school day. Therefore, we must recognize the importance of both consumption and production externalities in education and realize that the effects of education carry over to benefit society as a whole. We cannot, however, and should not count on education and schools to solve all the problems of ignorance, poverty, and prejudice in the world. By focusing our analysis on the education system, we run the risk of defining too narrowly the problems of reform. Social reform must take place throughout all social institutions, not only in the schools. We are deeply concerned here with the development of human capital, defined as a set of skills to allow a person to live a fulfilling, happy life. It is apparent that the chief public instrument in the production of human capital, namely, the system of formal education, functions with great unevenness across social classes. The Fleischmann Commission reported as follows in its study of the New York schools:

> The biggest problem in the state is the high correlation between school success or failure and the student's socio-economic and racial origins. The higher on the socio-economic scale a child is, the more likely he is to succeed in school. While children from affluent backgrounds score well on standardized tests, graduate from high school and attend college, children from low-income and minority backgrounds fail in school in numbers which far exceed their proportion of the state's total population. In spite of high expenditures and quality improvements, New York State is not providing equality of educational opportu-

nity to its students as long as the pattern of school success and school failure remains closely tied to a child's social origin.[11]

It seems both impractical and unproductive to assume that educational reform alone can break the tie between school success and social origin; the contribution of other public programs toward breaking the tie must be considered.

We pose a question to illustrate this point. If a child is having difficulty learning to read because of a correctable vision problem, is it not sensible to test a new pair of glasses on him before hiring a reading specialist to aid him? Clearly, a number of factors, not simply instructional personnel, affect a child's reading ability. Similarly, but on a more abstract level, we may postulate that an individual's capacity to learn (that is, to absorb additional human capital investment) is influenced by the quality of formal educational services available to him and the amount of learning he has achieved in the recent past. His learning capacity is also affected by medical care, dental care, nutritional standards, opportunities for recreation, access to a quiet study area, the encouragement given him by his family and friends, and what outcome he can expect from academic success. Only the quality of education available to him is immediately affected by current educational reform efforts. Pressure from family and friends and personal incentives to learn stand somewhat outside the direct reach of public services generally. But these two variables are indirectly affected by public policies with respect to discrimination in housing and employment and with respect to income redistribution. The middle group of variables— medical care, dental care, nutritional standards, opportunities for recreation, and access to a quiet study area—are provided publicly to low-income citizens. Concentrating solely on education is likely to produce a set of policies that can never attack the problem of school failure head-on; thus economic rationality demands that other public services complementary to learning be treated as integral parts of any reform effort.

As Henry M. Levin has stated,

educational services must include far more than instructional services. To a certain degree, the various investment sources might represent substitutes for each other in producing capital embodiment. For example, good instructional services may be able to compensate for many of the educational inputs that the family would normally provide. Yet . . . instructional services are probably

[11] *Report of the New York State Commission on the Quality, Cost, and Financing of Elementary and Secondary Education* vol. 1 (New York: Viking Press, 1973), p. 4.

not substitutable for a protein or vitamin B deficiency, a need for eyeglasses, or a debilitating systemic infection. . . . Certainly the schools have made nominal efforts in these directions with their provision of minimal dental service, free or low-cost milk programs, school lunches, and so on. Both Title I of the Elementary and Secondary Education Act of 1965 and Headstart emphasized that the provision of such "life support" services were legitimate educational inputs. Yet their importance has been understated in the actual world of expenditures, where the lion's share of so-called compensatory monies is allocated to reduce class size and for remedial reading and other instructional specialities.[12]

High Level Specialization in the Public Sector

When we recognize how public services complement each other in developing human capital and that we must provide at least some of these services, we are immediately confronted with a problem of big-city finance. Our federalized public system tends to benefit the more affluent. They, more than other segments of the population, are able to choose their place of residence. In making this choice, they can select from among communities having a mix of local public services they prefer. Nevertheless, some rich households prefer to live in large cities. The costs associated with city life may be so high, however, that even moderately rich families cannot reap the benefits of high-level specialization in group consumption that is usually available in cities.

High-level specialization means provision of services that *in their details* are used only by a very small fraction of the population. The only feasible way to provide such services in the public sector (high costs necessitate providing these services in the public sector) is to spread the costs over a very large population. Libraries serve as a good example. In general, the largest library is the best reference library. Suppose a city of 5 million inhabitants taxes itself at $1 a head for a library. This sum would cover the cost of purchasing about 100,000 books annually. Thus, the book budget for this city's library would allow it to acquire all the new books published in the United States and some books published abroad. Over the years such a library would house a collection of recorded knowledge and literature of inestimable value. On the other hand, suppose a suburb of

---

[12] Henry M. Levin, "Equal Educational Opportunity and the Distribution of Educational Expenditures," *Education and Urban Society,* 5 (February 1973): 161–62.

100,000 residents taxes itself at $1 a head for a library. This suburban library could purchase perhaps 2,500 books a year, or only less than 10 percent of the literary output of the United States.

High-level specialization also occurs as large cities provide themselves with diversified types of secondary schools, municipal universities, orchestras, ballet and opera companies, museums of art, history, and science, amusement parks and zoos, astronomical laboratories, botanical gardens, repertory theaters, architectural preserves, and so on. The great urban center still caters to the intellectual; it is the natural working and living place of many painters, sculptors, writers, poets, dramatists, composers, scientists, inventors, and performing artists. This wealth of talent must be readily accessible to those who can respond to it, and especially to young people, so that the creative process can continue to everyone's benefit.

Summary

Current discussions about educational reform stress the need for reducing disparities in providing funds for schools. As David Stern has written:

> The present system of public school finance, far from helping to equalize educational opportunity, actually promotes inequality by letting wealthier families obtain larger amounts of money for the education of their children. They achieve this by clustering together in more or less homogeneous school districts, so as to pool their wealth and avoid paying for the education of less-affluent children. Reliance upon local districts to finance public schools thus enables affluent families to convert their physical capital into human capital for their children.[13]

There is another view of the same problem:

> A guiding principle of public operation . . . is equal treatment of equals. If a set of families enters a state park to go hiking, that group would be shocked indeed to discover that the scenic trails were reserved for its richer members and that only barren and rocky paths were held open for the poor. Nevertheless, our public schools operate in such a discriminatory way. Those who doubt this assertion might advantageously walk through Benjamin Franklin High School in East Harlem and then through South Commack High School in Suffolk

[13] David Stern, "Some Speculations on School Finance and a More Egalitarian Society," *Education and Urban Society*, (February 1973): 226.

County, Long Island. If this is not convenient, any inner-city high school could be compared with any high school in a suburban community where average family income is above $14,000.[14]

Educational reformers have pointed to grievous fiscal inequities. Litigation in California in 1971 drew attention to the fact that residents of a poor school district, Baldwin Park, had a school tax rate double that of nearby Beverly Hills. At the same time, students in Baldwin Park received less than half the school services given students in the wealthier district. Indeed, as this example indicates, some poor families pay a higher percentage of their incomes for schools than do the more affluent, but they receive a lower standard of services in return. Furthermore, disparities in tax rates, even though partly capitalized into the value of residential properties, affect nonparents in mischievous ways. They bear little relation to the distribution of social benefits.

We think these are serious problems, and we have worked on solutions to them. Additional problems, however, now demand our attention. Unless they are taken into account early, educational reform plans can be misdirected or even harmful to our society.

In this chapter we have suggested that an important objective of reform of the American educational system is the removal of financial barriers to the achievement of social class integration. Another important objective is to provide greater diversity in educational offerings and establish a greater degree of individual choice in their use. These additional objectives, as well as the standard objectives of reducing educational disparities and achieving rationalization of school tax-rate structure, we feel must be accomplished without laying onerous financial burdens on low-income groups. Moreover, they should be accomplished in full recognition of the complementary nature of all public services and the desirability of improving everyone's access to high-level specialization in the public sector.

What we suggest vitally concerns the quality of American life. We hope to provide the reader with a conscientious review of how educational policy is devised. Policy formulation does not yet have a strong empirical basis—we cannot accept its findings with total confidence. Little is known, for example, about how children's rates of learning can be changed; indeed, no one can accurately ascertain or measure how learning occurs in

[14] Charles S. Benson, "Foreword," in John E. Coons and Stephen Sugarman, *Family Choice in Education: A Model State System for Vouchers* (Berkeley: Institute of Governmental Studies, 1971), p. 3.

the first place. Nevertheless, because we can recognize gross irrationalities in our present educational system, some appropriate directions for policy change can be laid down with reasonable confidence. These directions can guide us now. And for the future we look to improved means of obtaining empirical evidence to provide new directions.

Appendix to Chapter 1
Common Features of Existing Education Finance Arrangements in the States

In 1971–72 thirty-eight states had (and still have) a system of educational finance that is basically the same.[1] It is called the foundation program plan. Before describing the plan, however, and what it is supposed to accomplish, we shall discuss the systems of the other twelve states that do not use it.

Connecticut, Delaware, New Mexico, and North and South Carolina, for example, have an arrangement according to which the state pays to the localities a fixed sum per public school student ($205 per student in 1971–72 in Connecticut), plus "categorical aid" (to be described subsequently). The local district must then balance its budget from property taxation. Such a program does little to ease the financial plight of poor school districts.

A few states—Massachusetts, New York, and Rhode Island are examples—operate under a plan whereby the state government shares in the costs of schools as determined by the locality, with the further provision that the matching grant ratio be higher in poor districts than rich. A poor district for example might receive 75 percent of its school funds from state revenue sources and a rich district only 25 percent. The funds allocated in this manner are called percentage equalizing grants. The financial program is so constrained with upper and lower ratios, however, and in the absolute amount of assistance permitted that the program, in effect, is really a foundation program plan.

A *fully operational* percentage equalizing plan, however, establishes a

[1] Thomas T. Johns, *Public School Finance Programs,* 1971–72 (Washington, D.C.: Government Printing Office, 1972), pp. 5 ff.

financial nexus between the state and local authorities. Any two districts that spend the same amount of funds per student have the same local tax rate; all districts spending greater amounts have higher tax rates. This system establishes a one-to-one relationship between school expenditures per student and local tax rate and is said to provide wealth neutrality. The plan is now called district power equalizing and is discussed further in Chapter 3.

The Development of the Present System of Finance

The present approach to state aid for education stems from the work of the Educational Finance Inquiry Commission in New York State (1921–24). A volume of the commission's report was prepared by two Columbia University professors, George D. Strayer and Robert M. Haig; it offers what Paul R. Mort has described as the "conceptual basis" of present-day practice in equalization.[2] Sometimes the basic arrangement of state-local finance is described as the "Strayer-Haig formula"; alternatively, it is called the "foundation program plan." With more or less important technical modifications, this fiscal device still determines the allocation of school funds to local districts in the majority of states today.

In describing the practice of New York State in the early 1920s, Strayer and Haig stated: "A precise description of the basis upon which federal and state money is apportioned among the localities is an elaborate undertaking. The present arrangements are the product of a long history of piecemeal legislation. The result is chaos." The authors did provide, however, the following summary:

> Almost all of the state aid is distributed primarily on a per-teacher quota basis which varies with the classification of the school district and, in the case of one of the quotas, with the assessed valuation in the district. Approximately one-half of the state aid is entirely unaffected by the richness of the local economic resources back of the teacher, and the position which is so affected is allocated in a manner which favors both the very rich and the very poor localities at the expense of those which are moderately well off.[3]

[2] George D. Strayer and Robert M. Haig, *Financing of Education in the State of New York,* A Report Reviewed and Presented by the Educational Finance Inquiry Commission Under the Auspices of the American Council on Education (New York: Macmillan Co., 1923). Paul R. Mort's statement appears in Paul R. Mort et al. *Public School Finance,* 3rd ed. (New York: McGraw-Hill Co., 1960), p. 203.

[3] Strayer and Haig, *Financing of Education,* p. 162.

In moving toward their recommendation for a new fiscal arrangement, Strayer and Haig first stated:

> There exists today and has existed for many years a movement which has come to be known as the "equalization of educational opportunity" or the "equalization of school support." These phrases are interpreted in various ways. In its most extreme form the interpretation is somewhat as follows: The state should ensure equal educational facilities to every child within its borders at a uniform effort throughout the state in terms of burden of taxation; the tax burden of education should throughout the state be uniform in relation to tax-paying ability and the provision of the schools should be uniform in relation to the educable population desiring education. [4]

This has a modern ring as far as the prescription about tax burden goes. It is no longer possible, however, to believe that "equal educational facilities" represent "equal educational opportunity." It is now recognized that equality of purchased inputs does not, on the average, produce equality of educational outputs among the different groups of our society. That is, it is recognized today that the learning requirements of one student may differ from those of another; thus an educational program that allows one student to develop his abilities to a high degree may be more or less expensive than a similarly effective program for another student.

Nevertheless, let us proceed with the development of the Strayer-Haig formula.

> To carry into effect the principle of "equalization of educational opportunity" and "equalization of school support" . . . it would be necessary (1) to establish schools or make other arrangements sufficient to furnish the children in every locality within the state with equal educational opportunities *up to some prescribed minimum* [emphasis added]; (2) to raise the funds necessary for this purpose by local or state taxation adjusted in such manner as to bear upon the people in all localities at the same rate in relation to their taxpaying ability; and (3) to provide adequately either for the supervision and control of all the schools, or for their direct administration, by a state department of education. [5]

Note that the authors have now replaced "equal educational facilities" with the notion of "equality up to some prescribed minimum." They suggest also that some schools may be directly administered by the state department of education. One of the drawbacks of educational practice is that a school that is obviously and grossly failing to meet the needs of its

[4] Ibid., p. 173.
[5] Ibid., pp. 174–75.

students is allowed to continue under the same local district management year after year. This particular suggestion of Strayer and Haig has not yet been given enough attention.

Next, the proposal for the new system of state-local finance was formulated:

> The essentials are that there should be uniformity in the rates of school taxation levied to provide the satisfactory minimum offering and that there should be such a degree of state control over the expenditure of the proceeds of school taxes as may be necessary to insure that the satisfactory minimum offering shall be made at reasonable cost. Since costs vary from place to place in the state, and bear diverse relationships to the taxpaying abilities of the various districts, the achievement of uniformity would involve the following:
> 1. A local school tax in support of the satisfactory minimum offering would be levied in each district at a rate which would provide the necessary funds for that purpose in the richest district.
> 2. This richest district then might raise all of its school money by means of the local tax, assuming that a satisfactory tax, capable of being locally administered, could be devised.
> 3. Every other district could be permitted to levy a local tax at the same rate and apply the proceeds toward the cost of schools, but
> 4. Since the rate is uniform, their tax would be sufficient to meet the costs only in the richest districts and the deficiencies would be made up by State subventions.[6]

An example may help clarify the plan. Suppose it is determined that a satisfactory offering costs $1,200 per student per year. If the richest district has an assessed valuation of $40,000 per student, then a levy of $3 per hundred of assessed valuation will finance the school program in the richest district. All districts would be expected to tax themselves at the $3-per-hundred rate or higher. Every district but the richest would receive some state aid, just enough to meet the deficiency between the yield of the $3-per-hundred levy and the cost of the minimum offering. A district with $39,000 of assessed valuation per student would receive $30 per student from the state. Likewise, a district with only $2,000 of assessed valuation per student would receive from the state $1,140 for each of its students. Thus all districts could provide the minimum offering while paying a local tax at no higher rate than would be paid for a $1,200 program in the richest district.

⁶ Ibid.

Some Imperfections in Application of the
Strayer-Haig Formula

In practice, the Strayer-Haig system of state-local finance has a number of drawbacks:

States that use the plan often leave their school districts in a relatively unequalized condition. That is, some low-income districts find it necessary to levy a local tax at a high rate to produce a low-expenditure (per student) program, while at the same time rich districts are able to provide themselves with high expenditures (per student) at low tax rates. Thus the relation between quality of school program provided in different districts (as measured by dollar expenditure per student) and local tax effort is inverse, not direct.

This fiscal device, whose chief object is "equalization," fails so notably to achieve equity for at least three reasons:

1. The dollar value of the minimum educational offering is commonly set so low that many districts, rich and poor alike, find it necessary to exceed it. Above the value of the minimum offering (or foundation program) the interdistrict differences in assessed valuation per student have their full effect. Suppose, for example, the value of the minimum offering is $1,200 per student. Two districts, A and B, each elect to spend $1,600 per student. Let assessed valuation per student in A be $20,000 and in B $5,000. The extra tax rate effort to advance expenditures from $1,200 to ·$1,600 per student is $2 per hundred in A and $8 per hundred in B. Suppose B could advance its rate only by $4 per hundred, taking into account local fiscal realities and possible legal constraints imposed by tax limitations. It would then have half the supplementary program of A at twice the supplementary tax rate.

2. The local contribution rate is seldom set at the rate that would pay for the foundation program in the richest district. Given the very unequal distribution of nonresidential properties, the richest district (on the basis of assessed valuation per student) is likely to be very rich indeed, and the mandatory local contribution rate would be very small. The result in a literal reading of the Strayer-Haig formula would be that the state government would be paying for almost all of educational services. To avoid this, a higher local contribution rate is selected than that which would raise the value of the foundation program in the richest district.

3. Theoretically, then, those rich districts that raise *more* than the

value of the foundation program per student at the standard local contribution rate should turn this excess over to the state for redistribution to poorer districts. The contrary happens, in that such rich districts are given a flat grant, or basic aid, for each student. The result is antiequalizing. Some might argue simply that equity would prevail if the flat grant were abolished. But then one must reckon with the fact that several of the boroughs of New York City are flat-grant districts for the purpose of computing state aid for education.

Summary

In addition to equalization aid and basic aid, state governments fund wholly or in part several types of categorical programs—textbooks, school construction, transportation, school lunches, remedial reading, special services for the physically handicapped and mentally retarded, programs for educationally disadvantaged students, and so on. Specific procedures for allocating these funds vary widely from state to state. In order to avoid making our discussion as complex and unreadable as most states' educational codes, we will not examine these procedures here. The interested reader is referred to the code of his own state, and we strongly suggest a chilly room and a stiff chair before submersion.

On a more empirical basis then, state aid to local school districts can be reduced to the following formulas:

Total State Aid = Equalization Aid + Basic Aid + Categorical Aid
         where
Equalization Aid = Guarantee − Basic Aid − (Minimum or
                  Computational Tax Rate × Assessed Valuation
                  per pupil)

2

HOW WE GOT WHERE WE ARE

IN EDUCATIONAL REFORM

We are not unique in recognizing that the schools need changing. During the past two decades, school reform has become a subject of much interest; the large volume of popular books and articles on the subject testifies to this fact. The reform effort, however, is not easily classified or described. The variety of reform proposals, as well as the variety of problems they attempt to solve, is perhaps the most striking characteristic of the movement. Though we are primarily concerned with financial and organizational reform in education, we must first outline some other threads in the reform story—revisions in the teaching-learning process, the attack on educational failure, and the search for an educational technology. Not only are these efforts interesting in themselves, but their results have largely shaped the current pattern of educational reform.

Revisions in the Teaching-Learning Process

Curriculum reform, or revision in the teaching-learning process, has been proceeding on a number of fronts during the past fifteen years. Improvements in teaching style and curricular materials have, of course, always been incorporated into American classrooms. But the curricular reform movement seemed to take a different turn in the late 1960s with the publication of three books: Herbert Kohl's *36 Children,* Jonathan Kozol's *Our Children Are Dying,* and John Holt's *Why Children Fail.* These books

25

mark important milestones of the school reform movement for a number of reasons. First, they were widely read outside of the traditional educational establishment; that is, parents and other concerned citizens were suddenly confronted by the realities of the educational system their children faced every day. Second, these books did more than catalog the schools' educational failures; they startled people with the knowledge of the schools' failures to achieve racial and social class integration. Third, these and other books clearly revealed that many students were not only learning poorly or not at all, but that they were also bored and dissatisfied with their schools; they were more and more alienated from the process of learning and skeptical of the opportunities provided them by their schools and teachers.

Probably the greatest impact of these books, and the many others that followed in their wake, has been to increase the awareness of the average citizen about the situation of schools in his or her community. At the same time, they have had a marked effect on the educational establishment, especially in the development of programs like the "Right to Read Effort" and in innovations like the "open classroom" and the community-based high school.

The national Right to Read Effort, first articulated at a Washington, D.C., conference in 1970, developed in response to the startling discovery that large numbers of students graduated from American public high schools without knowing how to read adequately. To attack this problem, state education departments set up task forces designed to upgrade reading programs in the schools and develop better methods of training teachers in reading instruction. Though we cannot proclaim with certainty American students no longer have a "reading problem," the Right to Read Effort at least focused much needed attention on reading failure. It provided the necessary incentive to make state educational officials respond to the problem with a number of new solutions.

Another curriculum reform that has been recently publicized is the movement toward the informal or open classroom. These classrooms, usually at the elementary level, are based on the model of the British infant schools which resemble American kindergartens. In such a classroom learning is individualized; a student works on a project that interests him or her and the teacher acts as a resource person rather than as the director of the learning process. Individualized instruction is a goal toward which most good teaching strives—each child should proceed at his or her own pace and according to individual abilities. The informal classroom goes even further toward individualization, however; it actually tailors the content of education to a child's tastes.

The impact of informal educational programs on academic and social success has not really been adequately measured, largely because reform is recent. Also, no single generation of children has spent the entire period of schooling in informal classrooms. The movement toward informal classrooms has significantly altered the shape of elementary education for the coming decade, however, and probably has had some effect on most teachers and students.

While elementary education has felt the impact of informal educational programs, secondary education has experienced some major thrusts of reform. In community-based high schools, such as the Parkway Program in Philadelphia, students do some portion of their work outside conventional classrooms. A student interested in communications, for example, might take a course for credit at a local radio station; another student might work at an automotive repair shop. Similarly, a student having a more specialized intellectual interest, perhaps a compelling desire to learn about American society during the 1920s, might be able to take a course on this subject at some local university or community college.

In addition, course offerings in most community high schools are based on student interest. If a number of students are especially fascinated by a certain historical period or a specific subject (such as the importance of the whaling industry in American history), they would try to find an instructor who is knowledgeable on this subject; if student interest were widespread enough, a course would then be offered. Required high school subjects are also offered, of course, by a core teaching staff in most community high schools. But even these subjects are slightly different from their counterparts in more traditional settings. An English course, for instance, might concentrate on South American literature or journalism; a history course on the women's rights movement or on the Civil War.

Two premises underlie the operation of community high schools. First, students can successfully learn from actually doing things; therefore, education should not be divorced from reality. Second, there should be a degree of consumer choice in education. If an elective course is offered and no one is interested in the topic, then no one should be forced to attend. The advantages are obvious: students are more interested in their studies when they are doing something they enjoy. We think it perfectly reasonable to give high school students, many of whom are mature and thoughtful about their interests and aptitudes, more responsibility for their own education.

The Attack on Educational Failure

Along with the curriculum reform movement, another effort has developed. The attack on educational failure, as we shall call this effort, is aimed especially at those children who are having difficulty in school.

Many special programs have always been provided for children who are having difficulty in school. For well over a decade cities such as New York and St. Louis have operated such special programs. In 1965 the California legislature passed the Miller-Unruh Basic Reading Act to provide additional resources in the early grades to children having difficulty in learning to read. The real attack on educational failure though, came with passage of Title I of the federal Elementary and Secondary Education Act in 1965. Ralph Tyler described the general objective of Title I:

> The conditions of life today require the education of everyone who would participate fully in it. At least 15 per cent to 20 per cent of our children are not now attaining the level of education for employment, for intelligent citizenship, for responsible parenthood or for achieving their own individual potential. These disadvantaged children include those with one or more of various kinds of educational handicaps arising from a variety of physical, educational, cultural and emotional conditions. The children are distributed throughout our country, but the particular patterns of handicaps vary widely among the schools. The task for each of us is to study the disadvantaged children in our own school, seeking to understand their handicaps and then to work out a comprehensive program for the school, a program that is calculated to make an effective attack upon the problems these children face and that uses the resources available to the school.[1]

The introduction of Title I recognized a great need for compensatory programs designed to attack educational failure. But, in our opinion, from its beginning Title I has operated under two handicaps. First, funds are rarely targeted toward solving specific educational problems or ensuring that the extra resources provided are actually spent on disadvantaged students. Instead, political pressures make it likely that resources are distributed more broadly over an entire school district, thus defeating the purpose of the act.[2] Second, excessive localism is a problem. That is, practically all

---

[1] Ralph Tyler, "The Task Ahead," in U.S. Office of Education, *National Confeence on Education of the Disadvantaged* (Washington, D.C.: Government Printing Office, 1966), p. 63.

[2] This is the position taken in two authoritative works: Stephen Bailey and Edith Mosher, *ESEA: The Office of Education Administers a Law* (Syracuse, N.Y.: Syracuse Univer-

the federal money for disadvantaged students is dispensed by school districts. This procedure is based on the assumption that school district authorities know what actions to take to improve the learning rates of disadvantaged students, the target group for Title I funds. On the contrary, district officials may not even be aware of the nature of the educational failure they are trying to correct. In addition, this distribution method assumes that local school districts are able to direct the creation of a supply of resources to overcome learning failure. Actually, most school districts do not have a cache of alternative programs to overcome the failure of existing methods and programs. If the alternatives were there, Title I would not be needed to develop them.

This does not mean that Title I has had no positive effect. Before its passage in 1965 educators in general had assumed that the goal of education is to equalize inputs, that is, to ensure that the educational resources available in schools were the same. As this equalization of inputs was accomplished, it was assumed that children with the best minds and talents would be identified from all social classes. In other words, equality of purchased inputs would produce roughly equal distributions of educational outputs in each social class.

The Title I philosophy denied this assumption. It said instead that social class considerations complicated the educational input-output equation. The act proposed that *additional* financial resources were needed to make certain that the talents of children from lower socioeconomic classes were discovered and developed by the schools. Since low-income families are concentrated in certain districts and their children attend certain schools, some believed it was imperative for government to expend additional resources in these districts and schools. In 1965, then, the educational establishment was finally confronted by the fact that the educational system was not really acting as the great balancing wheel of society; something had to be done if the schools were to help erase social class segregation.

The problem with Title I was not its theory but its practical execution. Once the Title I philosophy was accepted by most educators, they felt that their only commitment was to inject more dollars into programs for educationally disadvantaged students. Although money per se is a necessary condition for educational progress, it is not the only condition. What was

sity Press, 1968), p. 119; and John Hughes and Anne Hughes, *Equal Education: a New National Strategy* (Bloomington: Indiana University Press, 1972), pp. 44-48.

needed and yet lacking was a hard look at the *kind* of educational programs being provided to raise the achievement level of the disadvantaged. School officials should have asked themselves questions like these: What special talents should teachers and other instructional staff have in order to help overcome the educational disadvantages of their students? How can persons with these special talents be found, trained, and then induced to work in inner-city schools? Are special educational facilities really useful? How and where should they be provided? How long would it take to acquire at least a minimum of these special resources, both human and material, and deliver them to disadvantaged students? What should be done meanwhile? Do children in some geographical areas need more and different resources than other children? What postsecondary opportunities should be provided for the generation of low-income students educated under the new programs of Title I?

Unfortunately, such questions were seldom asked, and the response to Title I was simply to pour more money into districts or schools having large proportions of disadvantaged students. At the same time there was no requirement that the money be directed solely at these students or concentrated in programs that had proved their effectiveness. As it turned out, Title I programs in most states, except possibly Michigan, are viewed at best as a mixed success. The inability of Title I to counter educational failure and the resulting skepticism of many educators and politicians about similar reform efforts have had a marked effect on the progress of other educational reforms. We will return to this point later in the chapter.

The Search for Educational Technology

While educators sought to revise the teaching-learning process and politicians tried to attack educational failure with massive inputs of money, another group of reformers was searching for educational technology. Beginning in the late 1950s educators were urged to discover schemes of instruction that were more effective, or "cost effective" as some would say. Many programs claiming greater efficiency have been devised: team teaching, language laboratories, modular scheduling, computer-assisted and managed instruction, educational television, the development of a cable-television network. No matter what the innovation is, the essential objective is either to increase specialization of labor used in schools or to substitute physical for human capital.

Unless definite steps are taken, we can expect the costs of school management and instruction to rise steadily. In 1967 William Baumol of the Department of Economics at Princeton University, described the difficulty in controlling costs in education. He observed that productivity increases occur unevenly over the components of our economy. Productivity increases are likely to be low when labor bulks large in the productive process, as it does in education. Conversely, in components of the economy in which physical capital is more important than human capital, such as manufacturing, technological improvements can proceed at a more rapid pace, and productivity can rise at a relatively high rate. Baumol states: "Thus the very progress of the technologically progressive sectors inevitably adds to the costs of the technologically unchanging sectors of the economy, unless somehow the labor markets in these areas [for, say, teachers' services] can be sealed off and held absolutely constant, a most unlikely possibility." With respect to education Baumol adds: ". . . as productivity in the remainder of the economy continues to increase, costs of running the educational organizations will mount correspondingly, so that whatever the magnitude of the funds they need today, we can be reasonably certain that they will require more tomorrow, and even more on the day after that." [3]

Up to this point technology has not brought about major changes in teaching methods, although it has had a marked effect on school management. It has helped simplify processes like the planning of facilities, menu planning, site selection, class and bus scheduling, and other large-scale planning efforts. A number of factors explain the limited role of technology in instruction. Technological equipment is too expensive; local districts are understandably reluctant to invest money in hardware (computers, television, cassette systems) without being certain that imaginative curricular materials will be available to be used in conjunction. Private companies that produce technological materials, or "software," have not really plunged into the educational market, since they have more profitable and expansive markets in other areas.

Moreover, much of the material that has been developed is neither very imaginative nor exciting. In many instances educational materials designed for use with technological aids are *preprogrammed*. Using a technological aid, a child may study an interesting subject and proceed at his or her own

[3] William Baumol, "Macroeconomics of Unbalanced Growth: The Anatomy of Urban Crisis," *American Economic Review* 57, no. 3 (June 1967): 415–26.

pace; but the student is still following somebody else's prescribed course and is expected to give predetermined answers. A math machine, for example, includes an assignment in giving change. The question is asked: How can one give change equal to seventy-five cents? The only answer the machine will accept is "one half-dollar and one quarter"; "three quarters" is considered an incorrect answer!

Improved methodology could most likely solve the problem in this example, but better programming methods would not alter the fact that the correct answer to a programmed question will always be the expected answer. The unfortunate effect of such overprogrammed materials is that children lose their creativity and simply assume that learning means giving the correct (that is, the anticipated) answer.[4]

Another factor explaining the limited role of technology in instruction is that educational innovations are not readily exportable from one school setting to another. A teaching tool that is effective in one school may show poor results in another school, or even within the same school at a later time. This occurs because technological methods now used are greatly influenced by an instructor's individual teaching style. Since no one really understands teacher-student interaction, technological materials are still very dependent on the way a specific teacher incorporates these materials into a specific educational setting. Thus school officials are reluctant to channel time, money, and energy into the development of technological teaching methods when they cannot be sure that these methods will be effective from one year to the next or from one classroom to another.

The discussion of educational technology, curriculum reform, and the development of Title I in the context of the history of educational reform are important for this reason. The inability of educators and politicians to raise educational achievement, either generally or specifically in relation to disadvantaged students, has slowed down the reform effort. It has made many people skeptical of large-scale educational change. Unfortunately, this negative outlook seems to pervade popular thinking about educational reform and has brought the reform effort into the courts and political arenas of state legislatures. Without initiative from these bodies, especially in the areas of finance and organization, we can no longer assume that the structure of education will change. In addition, it became clear that curriculum reform without simultaneous financial and organizational reform did little

---

[4] For a more complete discussion of educational technology see Mark Gerzon, *A Childhood for Every Child* (New York: Outerbridge and Lazard, 1973), pp. 163 ff.

to change the way schools operated. We will now describe how the issue of educational reform actually got into the courts in the first place.

Documents of the Finance Reform Movement

After World War II the chief task of the American educational system seemed to be that of providing additional physical facilities for the millions of new students who turned up at the door of the schoolhouse. Indeed, educational administrators were apparently trained to place much greater emphasis on "winning school bond elections" than on assessing the content of educational programs or the equitable treatment of students from different social classes.

By the 1970s, however, the pressure of rising enrollments has subsided. Educational administrators are less concerned with seating space than with making sure that all students have access to the kind of education that best suits their needs. This change in outlook did not happen overnight, nor was it accomplished without a great deal of thought. It is much easier, after all, to erect more school buildings than to develop positive educational programs that attack social and racial segregation and educational failure. This new reform mentality probably began around 1955 with the discoveries that educational offerings varied tremendously from school district to school district, and that poor districts usually provided poor education.

By 1955 the training of educational administrators had come to include field activity in which faculty and graduate students together prepared a local development plan for a contracting school district. At Harvard, for example, some of the districts involved were situated in the older industrial cities of New England; some were located in affluent suburbs. The contrast discovered in public provision in rich and poor districts was striking. In 1957 in Pawtucket, Rhode Island, the Harvard Center for Field Studies found fourteen school buildings, some of which served physically handicapped students, so unsafe that it issued a mid-year emergency report recommending that they be closed. Among other hazards, buildings lacked exterior fire escapes and sprinkler systems, had boiler rooms without fireproofing, sagging interior staircases, exposed wiring, faulty electrical connections, and dead-end corridors.[5] After the Harvard report was issued the

[5] Center for Field Studies, Graduate School of Education, Harvard University, *Pawtucket* (Cambridge, Mass.: The Center, 1957), pp. 243–45.

city relocated the children out of the substandard buildings. By contrast, suburban school buildings visited by the Harvard study teams were generally safe; many of these schools offered varied instructional activities. Perhaps more important, differences in physical facilities between urban and suburban schools seemed to correspond with the quality of the educational program in each area.

The evidence of educational inequality uncovered by the Harvard study and other studies was almost impossible to ignore. In 1961 James B. Conant described the metropolitan areas of New York, Chicago, Detroit, Philadelphia, and St. Louis:

> I am convinced we are allowing social dynamite to accumulate in our large cities. I am not nearly so concerned about the plight of suburban parents whose offspring are having difficulty finding places in prestige colleges as I am about the plight of parents in the slums whose children either drop out or graduate from school without prospects of either further education or employment. In some slum neighborhoods I have no doubt that over a half of the boys between sixteen and twenty-one are out of school and out of work. Leaving aside human tragedies, I submit that a continuation of this situation is a menace to the social and political health of the large cities. . . . The contrast in money available to the schools in a wealthy suburb and to the schools in a large city jolts one's notions of the meaning of equality of opportunity. The pedagogic tasks which confront the teachers in the slum schools are far more difficult than those their colleagues in the wealthy districts face . . . [yet] in the suburb there is likely to be a spacious modern school staffed by as many as 70 professionals per 1,000 pupils; in the slum one finds a crowded, often dilapidated and unattractive school staffed by 40 or fewer professionals per 1,000 pupils. The contrast challenges any complacency we may have about our method of financing public schools. . . . [6]

In a somewhat later statement in 1965, Charles S. Benson indicated that the problem was indeed systemic and not confined to the dichotomy of urban ghetto versus suburban enclave. Writing about middle-sized New England cities, he said:

> In Brookline, Massachusetts, all elementary schools had a *school library* as early as 1951, except in one case where the children used a nearby public library. In his annual report for that year, and speaking of the establishment of a new library, the superintendent stated, "From November 13, 1950 (when the library at Lincoln School opened), to October 31, 1951, . . . there were

---

[6] James B. Conant, *Slums and Suburbs* (New York: McGraw-Hill Co., 1961), pp. 2–3.

15,901 experiences with books which [the] children would not have had if the Lincoln School library had not been established.'' In 1963, in Milford, Massachusetts, there were only 480 volumes for 365 students in the *junior high school,* and the library, manned only by student assistants, was open only two periods a day. Revere [Massachusetts] has not spent any public funds for school libraries in the last five years, and its expenditures on city public libraries are very low. There is a rather small room in the high school designated as a library, stocked presumably with books received as gifts, but it is used off and on as a classroom.[7]

Such contrasting conditions affect the capacity of each district to lure well-trained, hard-working teachers.

The . . . factors . . . of salary, class size, condition of buildings, and provision of auxiliary services have a strong influence on the size of the pool of applicants from which a district hires its teachers. . . . A teacher who is looking for a job will see that some districts pay much lower salaries than others do. Further, he will note that these are the same districts in which he stands a relatively high chance of getting stuck with an oversize class meeting in an old, run-down school building, where in any case, he will have relatively few auxiliary materials and services to make use of. Altruism aside, it is clear to which district he will send his application.[8]

The fact that some children were being taught noticeably. better than others did not necessarily mean that well-to-do-parents were bearing onerous tax burdens. Benson's presentation of the situation in California will illustrate further:

The . . . thing to realize is that some communities, the rich ones, are able to provide high-quality school programs at quite low tax rates. Beverly Hills has an enviable reputation both for the amount of money it spends on education and also for the wisdom with which the funds are spent. Yet, the 1962–63 budget brochure states, ''The new tax rate (for Beverly Hills' schools) still is the lowest in the State for a unified school district with an enrollment exceeding 600.'' And Beverly Hills' school taxes were 27 per cent lower than any other authority in Los Angeles County.[9]

Almost ten years later (1970–71) the tax rate in Beverly Hills was still one of the lowest of any unified school district in California—in Los Angeles

[7] Charles S. Benson, *The Cheerful Prospect* (Boston: Houghton Mifflin Co., 1965), p. 24.

[8] Ibid., pp. 24–25.

[9] Ibid., p. 27.

County only Santa Monica, a district of comparable size, had a lower rate—and Beverly Hills' expenditure level was still by far the highest of any unified school district in the county.

Soon after the shocking disparities in interdistrict provision had been exposed, educators began to realize that differences in provision existed within districts as well. Upon examining the schools within Detroit's school district in 1961, Patricia Sexton reported: "A typical upper-income child, then, goes to a school that is safer, more suitable and adequate for his needs, more attractive inside and out, with much better facilities in most subjects, including science, music, art, and library, and also with better lighting, lavatory, and other health facilities than the school attended by the average lower-income child." [10] As a particularly distressing incident of discrimination, Ms. Sexton noted that whereas 78 percent of elementary schools attended by upper-income children had free lunch and milk programs, only 58 percent of schools attended by very poor children (those from families having incomes below $3,000) had these programs.[11]

Thus during the decade from 1955 to 1965 there was a steady accumulation of evidence from different parts of the country showing that our educational system discriminated unfairly in the distribution of public resources. As a result, differences in educational provision existed between ghettos and suburbs, between poor and rich school districts of varying sizes, and among children living in different parts of a single school district. The evidence was certainly striking, but the response of public authorities was never strong enough to erase these disparities.

City governments, though, have managed to reduce some intradistrict disparities. Dollar expenditure per student in New York City, for example, is roughly the same among all schools at a given grade level; where differences exist among schools, they bear little relationship to the socioeconomic characteristics of the students attending these schools. Nevertheless, the distribution of teachers in New York City is still remarkably uneven. Schools attended predominantly by low-income students are more likely to have a higher proportion of a district's less experienced teachers than other schools; this inequity in the distribution of teacher talent continues in most large American cities in spite of rough equality of total educational expenditures.

The situation regarding interdistrict disparities, however, is less heart-

[10] Patricia Sexton, *Education and Income* (New York: Viking Press, 1961), p. 132.
[11] Ibid., p. 134.

ening. Even in late 1973 most state governments, who bear the responsibility to help solve this problem, had done little or nothing. For instance, in New York, long a leader in reforming educational finance, disparities in provision among districts seem to have worsened in the past ten years.

State inaction cannot be explained by citing an absence of reform proposals. By the mid 1960s many plans for reform were forthcoming. Among them were proposals for state assumption of the costs of teachers' salaries, state control of salary schedules, statewide property taxation, state-supplied aid-in-kind (such as services of reading specialists), tax base equalization, school-by-school reporting of pupil achievement, and the creation of exceptional schools in urban areas.[12] In truth, the role of the states in education and educational reform during the 1960s was wholly inadequate; not only did they fail to attack the general problem of educational inequities among districts, but they also did little to help large cities having educational problems of special magnitude. California, for instance, still has the largest categorical grant from its own revenue sources earmarked for urban education; yet this grant represents less than 2 percent of total state-local educational expenditures.

A state legislature should be able to design a workable reform plan geared to its own financial situation and the characteristics of its population. State inactivity in this regard, coupled with the seeming failure of traditional reform efforts, Title I, and educational technology to improve education significantly, has forced national and state courts to act for educational reform. The courts have chosen to concentrate on the issue of educational finance as a tool for change. This outlook, although reasonable, has somewhat standardized and narrowed the shape of possible reform, a subject we will turn to now.

The Legal Arguments

The first statement of the role of courts in educational reform is that of Arthur E. Wise of the University of Chicago. In *Rich Schools, Poor Schools* he compared court action to protect an individual's right to vote and obtain counsel with judicial action to ensure an individual's right to re-

---

[12] For a fairly complete set of recommendations in the mid-1960s, see Charles S. Benson et al., *State and Local Fiscal Relationships in Public Education in California* (Sacramento, Cal.: Senate Fact Finding Committee on Revenue and Taxation, 1965).

ceive an "equal education." With reference to the Equal Protection Clause of the Fourteenth Amendment, Wise indicated:

> In summary, what does equal protection mean? With respect to race and education, it means equal treatment in form as well as in fact, to the extent that the courts can enforce it. With respect to voting, it means one man, one vote, and with each vote, one value. With respect to criminal justice, it means equal treatment in form but, as yet, not in fact. So long as legal services are purchased in the open market, it is doubtful that the indigent will secure as good legal services as the wealthy. Herein lies a distinction between criminal justice and public education. In public education, all services are purchased by the government. At first glance, the availability of private education may seem to negate this distinction. . . . The concern here is solely with public education, which, unlike criminal proceedings, operates solely in the public sector. Therefore, it should be more possible to ensure equality in public education in fact as well as in form than it has been in criminal proceedings, because the purchaser is the government not the client.[13]

The argument that education represents a fundamental interest similar to voting rights and the right to counsel was subsequently laid out in greater detail by John E. Coons of the University of California Law Faculty and his colleagues William H. Clune, III, and Stephen D. Sugarman. They noted first that public education plays an important role in maintaining the American system of "free enterprise democracy." "No other governmental service can claim such a seminal role in preserving entry to and competition within the market. Man as competitor is first and foremost educated man: we do not expect him—indeed we do not permit him—to compete until he has been educated." They noted secondly, that a distinguishing quality of education is its compulsory nature. The poor, who lack the option of the rich to choose among a variety of private educational institutions, are required to keep their children in certain public institutions, possibly of an inferior character. This requirement, in many cases, is very confining, but it is unavoidable because education is compulsory. Thirdly, education is universally relevant. "Not every person finds it necessary to call upon the fire department or even the police in an entire lifetime. Relatively few are on welfare." Yet all people have a direct requirement to participate personally, face-to-face, in educational experiences. Fourthly, according to Coons and his colleagues, "Education is the only planned,

---

[13] Arthur E. Wise, *Rich Schools, Poor Schools: The Promise of Equal Educational Opportunity* (Chicago: University of Chicago Press, 1968), pp. 187–88.

continuing and universal relation with the state." Lastly, education is the service through which the state deals with a person as a person; they state that "it is public education that enters actively to shape that development [of a person] in a manner chosen not by the child or his parents, but by the state. When the state educates, it stamps its mold on the personality of the child." [14]

Based on these arguments, which establish a special importance for education among publicly financed services, one might assume that the state should bear exclusive responsibility for ensuring children the appropriate educational services they need. Coons and his colleagues maintain the contrary, however: if localism in controlling educational resources can be made compatible with fiscal equity, it is to be preferred over a state-operated educational system. "The citizen who is jealous of state prerogatives under the Constitution is likely also to cherish the 'prerogatives' of school district 52 over and against the state. The attitude is not only understandable but, within limits, laudable. It is usually supported upon the rationale [that] local people should support and run their own schools." [15] Such reasoning is said to be based on the principle of "subsidiarity," or local control.

As a response to the inequitable distribution of educational resources, Coons and his colleagues lay down the following possible judicial rule, called Proposition I: "The quality of public education may not be a function of wealth other than the wealth of the state as a whole." [16] According to them, this rule is satisfied if the state establishes a system of "resource equalizing" grants, for example. These would ensure that any two school districts choosing to levy the same local tax will have available the same number of dollars per student to spend. This scheme, called district power equalizing, is one we will discuss more fully in Chapter 3.

The California Supreme Court, in its August 30, 1971, ruling on demurrer in the case *Serrano* v. *Priest* accepted Coons's arguments that public education represents a "fundamental interest." The court then declared that the California system of school finance was properly subject to "strict judicial scrutiny." It found, at least tentatively, that the California

---

[14] John E. Coons, William H. Clune, III, and Stephen D. Sugarman, "Educational Opportunity: A Workable Constitutional Test for State Financial Structures," *California Law Review*, 57 (April 1969): 387–89.

[15] John E. Coons, William H. Clune, III, and Stephen D. Sugarman, *Private Wealth and Public Education* (Cambridge, Mass.: Harvard University Press, 1970), p. 15.

[16] Coons et al., "Educational Opportunity," p. 311.

system allowed the distribution of educational resources to be unduly subject to a "suspect classification," namely, the taxable wealth of school districts. The court stated:

> Although the amount of money raised locally is also a function of the rate at which the residents are willing to tax themselves, as a practical matter districts with small tax bases cannot levy taxes at a rate sufficient to produce the revenue that more affluent districts reap with minimal tax efforts. . . . For example, Baldwin Park citizens, who paid a school tax of $5.48 per $100 of assessed valuation in 1968–69, were able to spend less than half as much on education as Beverly Hills residents, who were taxed only $2.38 per $100.

The court then concluded:

> For the reasons we have explained . . . the system conditions the full entitlement to such [fundamental] interest on wealth, classifies its recipients on the basis of their collective affluence and makes the quality of a child's education depend upon the resources of his school district and ultimately upon the pocketbook of his parents. We find that such financing system as presently constituted is not necessary to its attainment of any compelling state interest. Since it does not withstand the requisite "strict scrutiny," it denies to the plaintiffs and others similarly situated the equal protection of the laws. If the allegations of the complaint are sustained [upon retrial in lower court], the financial system must fall and the statutes comprising it must be found unconstitutional.

The *Serrano* decision thus established the main legal framework for accomplishing reform of educational finance. A number of similar cases followed *Serrano* in other states, specifically, *Van Dusartz* v. *Hatfield* in the United States District Court of Minnesota and *Rodriguez* v. *San Antonio Independent School District,* which was decided by a three-judge panel of the United States District Court for the Western District of Texas. As in California the *Rodriguez* judges ruled that the method of financing elementary and secondary education in Texas violated the Fourteenth Amendment. They granted state officials two years in which to devise a plan that would reallocate school funds to assure that children's educational opportunities, as measured by expenditures per student, were no longer a function of local district wealth, as measured by the value of locally taxable property per student. The Board of Education of Texas voted to appeal this decision to the United States Supreme Court.

On March 21, 1973, the United States Supreme Court decided the *Rodriguez* case and effectively stopped, at least temporarily, school finance reform through federal action. By a single vote the Court supported the constitutionality of the existing Texas financing system. The Court, though, did leave open the possibility of opposite findings in cases at the state level, a result that has had an important effect on reform efforts in many states.

The Present Situation

The majority decision in *Rodriguez* written by Justice Powell is based upon a two-part argument. First, the Court sought to determine whether the Texas system of school finance discriminated against a suspect class and whether education is a fundamental interest. A positive finding on either point would require the Court to examine Texas school finance laws under standards of strict judicial scrutiny. In regard to wealth discrimination, the first point, the Court asserted that it could not identify a disadvantaged class. It noted that because low-income people live in both rich and poor school districts, the finance system does not discriminate against a class of people whose incomes are beneath a designated poverty level. Second, the Court noted that there is no group who because of its poverty (in terms of income or property) is *completely* excluded, or absolutely deprived, from enjoying the benefits of public education.

The absence of absolute deprivation is important because in prior decisions utilizing wealth as a suspect classification—for example, the inability of indigent criminal defendants to obtain court transcripts, an indigent defendant's right to court-appointed counsel, imprisonment of indigents because of inability to pay a fine, and indigents' inability to pay large filing fees for running in primary elections—the Court ruled wealth discriminatory laws unconstitutional only because they *completely* excluded poor people from enjoying the benefits of exercising their constitutional rights.

The Court further asserted that the Equal Protection Clause does not require absolute equality under the law. Consequently, the Court reasoned, the presence of relative deprivation, defined as differences in expenditures among school districts, is not sufficient to identify a suspect class. Finally, although the Court recognized the relationship between district wealth and spending per student, it did not consider children in poor districts a class worthy of strict judicial scrutiny.

It is clear that appellees' suit asks this Court to extend its most exacting scrutiny to review a system that allegedly discriminates against a large, diverse, and amorphous class, unified only by the common factor of residence in districts that happen to have less taxable wealth than other districts. The system of alleged discrimination and the class it defines have none of the traditional indicia of suspectness: the class is not saddled with such disabilities, or subjected to such a history of purposeful unequal treatment, or relegated to such a position of political powerlessness as to command extraordinary protection from majoritarian political process.[17]

The Court then turned to the question of interference with a fundamental right, one afforded explicit or implicit protection under the federal Constitution. While stating that "nothing this Court holds today in any way detracts from our historic dedication to public education," [18] the Court argued that the importance of a service does not establish its status as a fundamental right. Nowhere does the Constitution explicitly guarantee the right to education. Nor could the Court find any basis for asserting that education is implicitly protected. Although the Court recognized the value of education for exercising rights explicitly guaranteed by the Constitution—for instance, free speech and voting—it found no basis for asserting that present minimum educational offerings (available to everyone) fell short of protecting explicitly guaranteed rights.

Thus having asserted that no fundamental right was at stake and no discrimination existed on the basis of suspect classification, the Court decided that it need not apply strict judicial scrutiny to Texas school finance law. On the contrary, the Court needed only to determine whether the Texas system showed some rational relationship to legitimate state purposes. On this question the Court noted that the Texas system was similar to systems used virtually in every other state. The power to tax local property for educational purposes is a long-standing prerogative of the state. Like the systems of most other states, the Texas system guaranteed a minimum statewide educational program while maintaining significant levels of local participation and control. Although expenditure disparities arose from geographical subdivision into school districts, such subdivision is also a state prerogative. Moreover, in Texas it had not produced purposeful discrimination against any group or class. In short, the Court judged the system to be a rational method to further legitimate state purposes. The Court admitted, however, that the Texas system is not perfect. Although it recognized

---

[17] *San Antonio Independent School District* v. *Rodriguez,* U.S. Supreme Court, No. 71–1332, March 21, 1973, p. 24.
    [18] Ibid., p. 26.

that superior finance systems could be constructed, it firmly asserted that the mere existence of better methods in no way implies unconstitutionality of existing ones. If the Court were to rule a system unconstitutional simply because superior systems could replace it, it would be playing the role of a legislature, a role the Court refused to assume.[19]

The dissenting opinion of Justice Marshall in the *Rodriguez* case counters the preceding arguments. He states that in "light of the data introduced before the District Court, the conclusion that the school children of property poor districts constitutes a sufficient class for our purposes seems indisputable to me." He further argues that the discrimination shown violates the Fourteenth Amendment even though there is no absolute deprivation of education: ". . . this court has never suggested that because some 'adequate' level of benefits is provided to all, discrimination in the provision of services is therefore constitutionally excusable. The Equal Protection Clause is not addressed to the minimal sufficiency but rather to the unjustifiable inequities of state action. It mandates nothing less than that 'all persons similarly circumstanced shall be treated alike.' *F. S. Royster Guano Co.* v. *Virginia,* 253 U.W. 412, 415 (1920)."

Justice Marshall's dissent also conflicts with the majority opinion that the state's interest in ensuring local control is attained under the Texas system. "It is an inescapable fact that if one district has more funds available per pupil than another district, the former will have greater choice in educational planning than will the latter." Furthermore, he argued that local control in Texas is an illusion. "The most minute details of local public education . . . courses . . . textbooks . . . qualifications necessary for teaching . . . procedures for obtaining certification . . . even the length of the school day" are all legislated by the state. Justice Marshall continued:

> It ignores reality to suggest . . . that the local property tax element of the Texas financing scheme reflects a conscious legislative effort to provide school districts with local fiscal control. If Texas has a system truly dedicated to local fiscal control one would expect the quality of the educational opportunity provided in each district to vary with the decision of the voters in that district as to the level of sacrifice they wish to make for public education. In fact, the Texas scheme produces precisely the opposite result. Local school districts

[19] For a more detailed discussion of alternative legal interpretations of the issues raised by *Serrano* and *Rodriguez,* including some used by the U.S. Supreme Court, see Paul A. Brest, "Interdistrict Disparities in Educational Resources," *Stanford Law Review* 23 (February 1971): 591–616.

cannot choose to have the best education in the State by imposing the highest tax rate. Instead, the quality of the educational opportunity offered by any particular district is largely determined by the amount of taxable property located in the district—a factor over which local voters can exercise no control.

Recent Developments in Other States

Despite the adverse United States Supreme Court ruling, legislation and litigation is proceeding at state levels, just as reformers anticipated after the *Rodriguez* decision. Just weeks after the *Rodriguez* decision was announced, the New Jersey Supreme Court reaffirmed an earlier decision in *Robinson* v. *Cahill:*

> Surely the existing statutory system is not visibly geared to the [state constitutional] mandate that there be a thorough and efficient system of free public schools for the instruction of all the children in this state between the ages of five and eighteen years. Indeed the State has never spelled out the content of the educational opportunity the Constitution requires. Without some such prescription, it is even more difficult to understand how the tax burden can be left to local initiative with any hope that statewide equality of educational opportunity will emerge. The 1871 statute embraced a statewide tax because it was found that local taxation could not be expected to yield equal educational opportunity. Since then the State has returned the tax burden to local school districts to the point where at the time of the trial the State was meeting but 28% of the current operating expenses. There is no more evidence today than there was a hundred years ago that this approach will succeed.

The court added, however, that once the state defines and offers an education according to its constitutional mandate, local districts might raise additional revenues "provided that such authorization does not become a device for diluting the State's mandated responsibility." On October 23, 1973, the U.S. Supreme Court declined to review the state ruling in this case.

Most states have constitutional clauses similar to the one in New Jersey, and, hopefully, successful claims can be made in state courts on this basis. The *Serrano* case was originally decided upon both state (California) and federal grounds, and state grounds alone may be sufficient to reaffirm the decision. The facts in the *Serrano* case are now being decided at the trial court level, since the California Supreme Court decided that there is cause for action and that the case must be reheard.

The state of California claims that a recent school finance bill passed by the legislature raises the foundation program level (guaranteed expenditure when a specified tax rate is levied) to an amount that is sufficiently high ($765 for an elementary school student and $950 for a high school student) to provide an adequate education for all children. Furthermore, California argues that it is not in the state's interest to equalize districts' ability to spend beyond the foundation level because there is disagreement over the worth of additional spending on education. Plaintiffs counter this last statement with the following argument: If there is uncertainty about what money can buy in education, why should only those in poor districts be placed at risk?

Plaintiffs point to large discrepancies between educational expenditures and the property wealth of districts. Because some 60 to 70 percent of the difference in expenditures is directly related to district wealth, even under the new legislation, they argue that as long as expenditures are based upon a local tax base, discrepancies of this kind will continue.

Two paragraphs cannot adequately summarize months of testimony before the trial court in the *Serrano* case. Even if the trial court supports the plaintiffs, the case will no doubt return to the California Supreme Court, which will probably then determine if the California constitution alone provides sufficient grounds to reaffirm its previous decision. California Supreme Court Justice Wright, who concurred with the majority decision in *Serrano,* has said, as reported in the *Sacramento Bee* of March 23, 1973, that state grounds might possibly determine the final outcome of *Serrano* v. *Priest.*

While the *Serrano* case was still in trial court, Governor Ronald Reagan promoted a Revenue Control and Tax Reduction Amendment to the California constitution that would have placed a lid on total state expenditures. Although the amendment was defeated in a special November 1973 election, it reveals serious dangers that might arise from similar proposals.

First, the amendment would have made it difficult for the state to respond to a court order affirming the *Serrano* decision. It is impractical to require high-spending districts to lower their expenditures in order to comply with *Serrano*. Instead political realities in California require that the expenditure levels of low-spending districts be raised. This "leveling-up," however, requires additional state funds; if the expenditure limitation amendment had passed, these funds would simply not have been available.

Without additional state money, school reform based on the outcome of *Serrano* could not have happened.

This amendment might have had a serious effect on year-to-year state funding of schools. If the amendment had passed in California, because the size of the state budget would have been controlled, state grants to school districts would not have grown even at their accustomed rate. Accordingly, the burden of meeting rising school costs and program expansion would have fallen on local districts. Authorizing the use of the local income tax by districts (a very cumbersome administrative process) would have required a two-thirds vote in the legislature. On the other hand, increasing local property tax limits would have required only a simple majority of the California legislature, and overriding these limits would have required only a simple majority of local voters. In addition, the state might have been tempted to cut back on some existing programs, such as free textbooks, thereby creating an additional burden on local tax bases. For these reasons, if the Revenue Control and Tax Reduction Amendment had passed, the local property tax would have been forced to bear the burden of increasing educational expenditure.

The British experience has shown that large programs, in terms of expenditures, are especially vulnerable under revenue limitation schemes. Modest adjustments in the budgets of such programs absorb large amounts of funds, ruling out the possibility of increases in many small programs. Therefore, coalitions of interest groups arm themselves to defeat budget increases in large programs and activities. Public education in California, a very large program, would be in an especially risky position. It is also locally administered. Thus if the initiative proposal had passed, the state legislature would have been pressed to shift incremental school financing back to the local authorities. This shift would result in heavier use of local property taxation, a step backward. Since local school districts are grossly unequal in taxable capacity, the invidious disparities in student support, somewhat ameliorated by recent legislation, would have quickly reappeared.

Spurred by court action, state legislatures have reentered the school finance issue. Recent legislation in Kansas and Florida, for example, has gone far toward equalizing school expenditures. We will discuss these and other developments in the Epilogue. Now, we will turn to the substance and shape of educational finance reform and examine the remedies proposed to erase educational inequalities.

3

THE SHAPE OF REFORM

Despite the setback in the United States Supreme Court's *Rodriquez* decision, we welcome the possibilities offered by a state-by-state response to education finance reform. Developing and implementing such reform is not easy, however. Under every proposed scheme some people will gain and some will lose; and if any scheme is to work, the losers must be reasonably appeased. Three major considerations underlie all efforts at reform: (1) the system should assure that the poor are not always on the losing side and should work to ameliorate racial and social class segregation; (2) the system should work more rationally than the present one; (3) the system should allow the consumers of education to make decisions, without regard to individual wealth, about the kind of education they want.

We will examine three proposed financing plans. They are based respectively on the premises that the state, the local community (that is, the school district), or the family unit should have the authority and responsibility for determining the amount of money spent on a student. Each alternative attempts to satisfy the criteria expressed in the California *Serrano* decision. In this chapter we will consider the advantages and disadvantages of two specific plans: *Full State Assumption* (FSA) in which the state has the financial decision-making power and *District Power Equalizing* (DPE) in which the local school district retains this power. In Chapter 5 we will describe a plan that gives the family unit decision-making power while assuring that the rich families will not have an advantage over poor families.

We are concentrating here on the decision to spend an amount of money, not on the decision about what to buy with this money. Like most educators, we simply do not and cannot know the best way to spend educational funds. Moreover, the consumer should have some choice among various educational offerings; therefore, we have no desire to standardize the educational process by mandating curricula or teaching methods. We recognize, however, that this does not mean that the purchaser of education can always have his way. Buying an education is somewhat like buying a car. We do not tell General Motors how to build a Chevrolet, although we may offer suggestions for improvements to be included in later models. Just as the consumer does not always know how to build a better automobile, he does not always know how to structure a better education. Even so, consumers should have the opportunity to express their feelings about the success of an educational system and, therefore, make the best "buy." At this point, we will concentrate on fiscal matters. In a later chapter we will begin to sketch a few of the possibilities that could be offered in a diverse educational market.

Full State Assumption

The simplest plan to ensure financial equality will control how much is spent at the state level. Clearly, spending equal dollar amounts on all children satisfies the *Serrano* principle of fiscal equity. But it does not satisfy important educational considerations, since different children have different educational needs. The state may recognize these different needs and still satisfy the equity principle, but it must do so uniformly across the state. If a state chooses such a financing plan, we say that it has assumed the full costs of public education, or adopted a full state assumption (FSA) plan. Under this plan a state can justify spending different amounts on different children in a variety of ways: it may stipulate that expenditures be different at different grade levels; it may recognize that to reach their potential children require costly compensatory and enrichment programs; it may see to it that children with physical, mental, or emotional handicaps have the benefit of special, though costly, programs and services; it may make available to children demonstrating special talents or simply keen interests specialized courses in science, art, or language; it may mandate that vocational and technical programs, though often expensive, be made available to students who desire them. A state may also take into account cost differences due to geographical location (for example, transportation costs of children who live far from school or the cost of buying air conditioners when a hot climate makes teaching and learning difficult). It may also take into account cost differences related to the fact that some districts must pay higher salaries than others to attract competent teachers. The basic premise of an FSA plan is not that all people will be treated identically but that people in similar circumstances will be treated similarly. The distribution of educational resources is based on two criteria: (1) learning requirements of individual students and (2) prices of educational goods and services (the purchased inputs of the educational process). Recognition of these two variables will cause the state to spend different amounts of money on different children.

The Structure of Full State Assumption

The first problem an FSA plan must address is how to rectify the pattern of expenditure differentials related to district wealth. The common approach is to level-up low-spending districts to a tolerable standard while requiring high-spending districts to forego further advances. Thus, the Fleischmann Commission's recommendation for full state funding specified that districts should be leveled-up to the sixty-fifth percentile of current expenditures per student in the districts of New York. Districts spending above that figure (in 1970–71, $1,143 per student) should be frozen and barred from further advances until the base rate for the rest of the state reached their own level. The Commission proposed further that all funds to pay for current operations should come from state sources, including funds to meet expenditures in high-spending districts. (That is, the high spending districts were to be "saved harmless" at state expense.) After about five to fifteen years the basic level of spending should advance through inflation to the point where all districts would be incorporated into a state-mandated, though not necessarily uniform, pattern of expenditure. The plan also specified that the state assume the cost of debt service for school construction and meet the full cost of new construction, with emphasis on improving physical facilities in high density areas.

As for differences in needs of students, it was specified that low achievers be assigned a value of 1.5 for distribution of educational resources, as compared with a value of 1.0 for achievers. It was indicated that most of the sums granted to help low achievers should be spent in the early grades, where basic learning patterns are set. In addition, a large sum (approximately $500 million annually) was to be made available to children with physical and emotional handicaps. The Fleischmann Commission was concerned that, for the time being, increases in spending should derive from clearly documented instances of need. Spending money in such a way would, hopefully, become a habit, and, accordingly, we would become more knowledgeable in identifying the needs of young people.

Regarding revenue, recommendations for full state funding ordinarily specify that the state impose a statewide property tax for schools. The Fleischmann Commission recommended such a tax at a rate of $2.04 per $100 of full valuation. This rate was determined to assure that the state would collect approximately the same amount that the localities had previously collected. Because some poor people live in property rich districts (which are likely to have their school taxes increased under a statewide property tax), it is important to incorporate a "circuit breaker" into full state funding recommendations. A circuit breaker is simply a fiscal device for ensuring that poor families do not pay an excessive amount of property tax relative to their incomes; details are give in Chapter 4.

In order to minimize the possibly harmful effects of centralizing the provision of educational services, full state funding plans may stress the importance of expanding the operations of regional educational authorities. By exploiting economies of scale, regional authorities can make available to students specialized courses and other services on an optional basis. This point is further discussed in Chapter 6. Similarly, full state funding plans may strengthen the autonomy of individual schools. The idea is that parents, staff, and students should have more power to decide what programs will be emphasized in a particular school and, in general, how the school's budget will be spent.

Under full state funding the driving force for raising the amount of money spent on public education is collective bargaining between organized teachers and the educational authority. Most sensibly, bargaining over major economic issues should occur at the state level. It is entirely appropriate that the bargaining officers for the state and a statewide teachers' union agree upon a regional pattern of salary differentials. In time this pattern of regional differentials would come to regulate the state's expenditures in the various local districts.

There is a major difference between full state funding and the present system. Under the present system the driving force to raise expenditures for education is local competition for resources—not collective bargaining as in full state funding. This local competition is an application, we might say, of the market mechanism in the public sector. It is sometimes suggested that we should not abandon the market mechanism altogether but should include within the full state funding plan a provision that local authorities can "add on" a sum (obtained from their local taxables) to the state-mandated expenditures. Ordinarily, it is stated that the add-on should have a definite upper limit; for example, it might be provided that the add-on could not exceed 10 percent of mandatory expenditures per student.

The Fleischmann Commission chose to offer a plan absolutely forbidding add-ons. The Commission believed that the richer, more educationally minded districts would use their influence in the state legislature to raise the amount of the add-on rather than to benefit the majority of school districts by raising the amount of the mandatory expenditures. Indeed, manipulation of the add-on could, over a period of years, serve to reproduce our present inequitable system of finance. Finally, the Commission held that arguments about the size of the add-on would probably distract both local authorities and the legislature from consideration of other serious educational issues.

District Power Equalizing

The idea of a wealth-equalized local add-on under FSA is another financing plan. Under this scheme local districts maintain a degree of control over the level of *local* spending, but, on the whole, revenues available to support educational programs are not based upon local wealth. Because district revenues are dependent upon local tax effort, this plan is called district power (or wealth) equalizing (DPE).[1]

(Another way to ensure equality of resources for equal tax effort is to redraw district boundaries so that all districts have the same wealth. Redistricting is not only impractical, but it is also highly unpopular politically. Furthermore, boundaries would have to be changed every few years to keep pace with shifting property values. DPE appears to offer the same

---

[1] DPE was first proposed in John E. Coons, et al., *Private Wealth and Public Education* (Cambridge, Mass.: Harvard University Press, 1970). It is closely related to "percentage equalizing grants," and these grants have had a long period of use in England. They were suggested for adoption in the United States by Harlan Updegraff in 1922. (For further discussion see Charles S. Benson, *The Economics of Public Education* [Boston: Houghton Mifflin Co., 1968], Chapter 6.) The essential argument made by Coons et al. is that percentage equalizing grants needs not be based on a strictly linear relationship between expenditures and local tax rates. Hence, DPE is the more flexible financial device, but both FSA and DPE have the equity feature that equal local tax rates produce equal spending per student, regardless of level of district wealth.

result with only a computational change, but it actually involves some side effects as we shall show.)

The following example illustrates a DPE plan. Table 1 shows a schedule of the revenue received by a district for *each* child when the district levies the tax rate corresponding to this expenditure level. This tax rate is levied regardless of how much money is actually raised by the local tax. If the district does not raise enough money to reach the basic expenditure level, the state makes up the difference. But if a district raises more than the guaranteed level, the excess is taken by the state for redistribution to poorer districts. Any district could choose an intermediate value of spending and tax rate; thus for a $625-per-pupil expenditure, the tax rate would be $1.25 per $100 full property value. Further details about DPE are given in the Appendix to this chapter.

Table 1   Example of DPE Proposal
Showing Tax Effort and
Corresponding Expenditure Level
for an Elementary Pupil

Expenditure per Pupil	Tax Rate per $100 of Full Property Value
$500 (minimum expenditure level)	$1.00
750	1.50
1,000	2.00
1,250	2.50
1,500	3.00

The expenditure levels in Table 1 support a basic program for a normal elementary school child. Just as in FSA, the state could assign values to the various types of children (high school, handicapped, educationally disadvantaged, and so on). Using values of 1.25 for high school students and 4.4 for blind students, for instance, each district would receive, for a $1 tax rate, $500 for *each* elementary student, $625 for *each* high school student, and $2,200 for *each* blind student. Expenditure levels corresponding to the higher tax rates could be similarly calculated.

Alternatively, funding for special students, say, for the handicapped or intellectually gifted, could be handled by providing fixed grants that are independent of the local decision on expenditure level.

Comparison of FSA and DPE

Neither FSA nor DPE is a perfect financing plan. In fact, the problems inherent in each scheme are troublesome and complicated. While we are fully aware of the criticisms and limitations of each plan, we believe that even more serious criticism can be directed at most school finance schemes now in use. Since some alternative is needed, we should examine the problems that are common to both plans.

One of the basic reasons for differences in spending among districts is, as we have pointed out, vast differences in district wealth. In the past the more affluent have banded together to exclude the poor from gaining the benefits of their superior tax base. While both FSA and DPE reduce the financial disincentive for districts to merge, it is still likely that small school districts (in some cases having fewer than fifty students) will exist under either plan. There is little educational justification for maintaining very small school districts except when population sparsity requires it. But many states recognize diseconomies of small scale and therefore give additional aid to these districts. Thus small school districts, often the wealthiest in a state, are placed at a financial advantage. We believe that this advantage hurts less wealthy districts and that small districts should be encouraged to merge for both educational and political reasons.

Both DPE and FSA preserve the structure of present district lines. These lines determine very closely the school or schools a child may attend but often have no rational basis as instruments of public policy. Alternative financing plans reduce the financial barriers to social class integration; but because they may not address the question of differential educational needs adequately, they may not succeed in removing them completely. Further, both plans ignore the burdensome responsibility of central cities to support many municipal services in addition to educational programs.

Some critics of DPE schemes argue that rather than simply not encouraging districts to merge, DPE will make it more likely for districts to divide. They argue that when districts can choose their educational system according to preference rather than tax base, various neighborhoods within large districts would want to claim autonomy and choose different educational expenditures. This has not been the case historically, though, because large districts have thus far been able to avoid division despite strong differences among neighborhoods and groups; New York City is a prime example of this. The division of districts is sometimes desirable, though. In fact, the districts of some cities, such as New York and Los Angeles, are far too large now. Breaking these giants into smaller units to promote greater local control while guaranteeing equal revenue-raising capabilities would appear to be a positive step.

Either DPE or FSA might decrease present reliance on the property tax to finance education. The minimum level of expenditure under DPE could be financed by any statewide tax, while the entire school bill under FSA could be raised statewide from nonproperty sources (primarily income and sales taxes). Considering the enormous amount of money currently raised through the levy on real property, however, it would be difficult to shift the burden completely to other statewide taxes.

DPE, unlike FSA, requires some kind of a local levy as a measure of effort. In most cases local districts would levy a tax on property to raise their share. This seems reasonable, since it would not be easy to administer an income tax on the basis of school districts. Moreover, a district income tax tends to breed more dishonesty than a property tax. Wealthy people could buy into recreational communities and claim this nonschool area as their residence; thus they could avoid a local income tax levied to support education. The property tax, on the other hand, cannot be so easily side-stepped.[2] Furthermore, the property tax is easily administered. Also, unlike income and sales taxes, property tax revenues respond sluggishly to economic patterns of boom and recession. Thus government is assured a stable source of revenue that facilitates budget planning. In short, there are good reasons for continuing to use the property tax for school finance, provided adequate measures are taken to protect low-income people from changes in property tax burdens (see Chapter 4).

The clear advantage of FSA over any other financing plan is the degree of equality achieved. Other plans that permit variations in local district spending open up the possibility that some children will be denied access to educational opportunities. Even if other plans eliminate wealth biases, only FSA eliminates discrimination on the basis of location.

On the other hand, a difficulty of FSA is that it assumes that the state can wisely decide what a good education is and how much it should cost. Once a state decides on a particular expenditure level, any lower expenditure deprives a child of a quality education; any higher spending level simply wastes the taxpayers' money. The real problem is that nobody is sure about the process of learning. Thus it is difficult effectively to assess

---

[2] For a further discussion of the administration of the property tax, see Charles S. Benson, *The Cheerful Prospect,* (Boston: Houghton Mifflin, 1965), Chapter 4.

class size, what kind of education and experience a teacher should have or what books and other educational tools should be used. Since nobody really knows what an "effective and efficient" education is, it seems almost impossible to determine how much it should cost. Any dollar amount established by an FSA plan will be based somewhat upon intuition and guesswork but mostly on politics. Moreover, the problem is further complicated when special needs and costs, as for vocational programs and programs for handicapped students, are considered. Presumably, some states would do a better job than others in deciding these matters. However, approaching educational reform strictly at the state level, where the current effort is chiefly directed, offers little hope for eradicating large interstate disparities in provision.

Perhaps the major point of debate on FSA involves its effect on local control of schools. Clearly, if the state is providing all the money for education, it may also choose to make all significant decisions about schools. But under any financing plan the state can impose so many program requirements that the only decision left for the school district to make, besides whom to hire, would be where to hold graduation if it rains. But the state might simply choose instead to mandate only the teaching of certain basic skills and leave all other educational decisions up to the local school district.

It is clear, however, that FSA severely limits the flexibility of local decision making by setting the spending level before the local district even decides upon the type of program it wants. Districts may want to provide special programs in ecology or the performing arts, for example, or to experiment with computer-assisted instruction or open classrooms. But a district's ability to implement such programs would not be dependent, as it is now, upon the willingness of local citizens to pay additional taxes. Instead the district would be forced to meet a predetermined budget and then see how much money is left for special programs. When the state pays for the total educational bill, some people fear that it is more likely to ignore local wishes and try to exercise too much control over how the money is spent. We do not share this fear, however, and instead trust that state education officials, in close contact with the political system, will remain aware of local tastes in education. Recently, there has been a noticeable trend in some states toward limiting state control over educational offerings while simultaneously increasing state aid for education.

Proponents of FSA counter these fears with the argument that their plan may actually expand local control. Under FSA, they claim, a school board would not have to concentrate on how to raise money. Rather it could be concerned with finding the best and most efficient ways to spend money.

Proponents of DPE state that under their plan the local district can state its demand for education by voting directly for it. There is no corresponding market mechanism included in an FSA plan. As long as the correct level of spending—that is, that amount purchasing the most efficient and effective education possible—remains unknown, a market mechanism provides important information to state government about consumers' evaluations of educational services. This argument does not reflect the whole truth, however. Up to now rich districts have set the tone of the education market since these districts usually consume more financial resources for their schools. For the most part, expensive equipment such as computer-assisted teaching machines, or the specialized services of certain teachers have been produced for the benefit of rich districts and are not equally useful to poor districts.

Under DPE there will no longer be any identifiable rich districts. However, there will most likely be a time lag before formerly poor districts can voice their market preferences as well as rich districts do now.

In any case, it is doubtful that residents of big cities are really able to express their desires for educational services by voting infrequently in a tax election. Having a choice about which public school within the city one's child attends might be a more effective market signaling device about educational preferences. Lastly, insofar as processes of local government reveal market demand by "voting with one's feet,"—that is, by choosing a town of residence that has an appealing set of services and an appealing tax rate—they are cumbersome and inefficient.

Likewise, proponents of DPE claim that their plan promotes efficiency in government, since under DPE a district must pay for every dollar it receives by raising its tax rate. Thus each district has a direct interest in achieving greater efficiency in its schools. Taxpayers' pressure for better management can have a positive effect on the way a district's educational system is run. Alternatively, it is felt by some, there would be little external pressure for efficiency in spending under FSA.

Again, we find this kind of argument not wholly convincing. Pressure toward efficiency conceivably could be much stronger under FSA, for the task under FSA is to squeeze as much educational output as possible from a given amount of resources. Thus, under FSA, educational aspirations in many districts will rise more rapidly than the state's financial allocations for them. The successful school administrator, therefore, will be the person who can make the most efficient use of resources in response to household demands. Under DPE, however, the successful administrator may be one who can most effectively swell the size of a budget that is possibly already wastefully large.

Enough has now been said to illuminate the fundamental dilemma underlying the design of reform proposals advanced in the wake of recent court decisions. Plaintiffs tend to uphold the value of subsidiarity, or local control. Based on this, they have suggested that a financial arrangement for DPE satisfies Proposition I as suggested by Coons and his colleagues: "The quality of public education may not be a function of wealth other than the wealth of the state as a whole."

A very important difference between FSA and DPE plans is that DPE allows, indeed encourages, the perpetuation of differences in educational provision. Such differences often have little rational connection to the needs or desires of school children, who are, after all, the primary (though nonvoting) clients of an educational system. DPE offers no more protection to children from apathetic or selfish adults than our present system does. It *may* break the connection between quality of education and size of local tax base, though, in the sense that high- and low-spending districts can no longer be generally identified by their taxable wealth. But at the same time, DPE allows districts to trade local tax relief (a benefit to resident adults) for financial starvation of the local schools. Thus if children are protected from the uneven distribution of locally taxable wealth, they are nevertheless vulnerable to possibly harmful influence of adult tastes for education services.[3]

Under DPE relative disparities in provision are tolerated in the name of an abstract principle, subsidiarity, and are, in a sense, advocated by public policy lawyers in *Serrano* and related cases. (This may explain why a majority of the United States Supreme Court did not view with great suspicion the relative disparities of our present, admittedly wealth-oriented, system). Subsidiarity is an important value. Local control of schools is a significant element of American democracy. In fact, the subsidiarity principle may partially explain why our present educational system is relatively well-financed, as we saw in Chapter 1. But as we have also shown, subsidiarity implies relative disparities of provision, disparities that could harm children who are offered inadequate school programs. A question must be

---

[3] Frank I. Michelman, "The Supreme Court, 1968 Term Forward: On Protecting the Poor Through the Fourteenth Amendment," *Harvard Law Review*, 83 (November 1969): 56.

asked: To what extent can we risk harming certain children in order to achieve the benefits of subsidiarity, which might include having a generally well-financed school system? This is a political judgment and, as such, can be made in the absence of quantitative data about the benign effects of local involvement in education. Posing the question this way, however, indicates that an alternative system exists which does not recognize subsidiarity—FSA has scant regard for the principle as expressed in the budget-balancing power of local districts. As to whether or not the system (as compared with DPE) would be risk free for children, FSA may reduce risk, but it by no means eliminates it.

To understand why FSA is not risk free, imagine two identical children, A and B. If A lives in a tight-money district and B in a generous one, under DPE A's education is at risk. FSA would remove A's disadvantage in relation to B, assuming, of course, that the educational needs of A and B are indeed identical. Now assume instead that A and B are not identical, that A requires many special services to attain full academic potential; in contrast, B needs only some special treatment. If A is not physically handicapped or poor, he or she is unlikely to get extra help under FSA—this will be the case until we can develop the scientific knowledge needed to tailor educational resources to the learning requirements of individual children who are considered normal.[4] If, on the other hand, A lived in an educationally progressive district under DPE, he or she would most likely be well cared for.

Therefore, we are led into a choice between two systems—one that emphasizes the rather vague value of subsidiarity and requires some degree of sacrifice on the part of some children (DPE), and another that is unconcerned with subsidiarity and ensures that all children will receive not less than some specified level of educational expenditure (FSA). Yet, because we cannot be certain about how much "more" a particular child may need, it is impossible to weigh the loss of subsidiarity under FSA—a loss that concerns us—against a potential of adequate response to children's special needs. When, moreover, districts retain power to allocate resources among alternative programs—and this power is generally preserved under most FSA plans—it can be claimed that students who desire some specific program not made available in the local district suffer from place discrimination in the same manner as they might so suffer under DPE.

[4] Similarly, the *Hobson* v. *Hansen* cases in 1967 and 1971 dealing with the distribution of school resources within the District of Columbia, though directed toward a glaring inequity, do not appear to allow much flexibility in making distinctions among students with respect to their learning requirements or personal tastes for educational services.

Categorical Aid

Some educational costs are really unrelated to the cost of a basic educational program. If a state institutes a finance plan that equalizes districts' abilities to support a basic education plan, local districts will still have to bear some considerable costs.

A few examples will illustrate our point. Transportation costs are usually higher in rural areas than in urban centers, because many children in rural school districts live at great distances from their schools. On the other hand, many costs are much greater in urban districts. As we have already mentioned, building new facilities in cities is very expensive, largely because of land scarcity and high property costs. Furthermore, the costs of vandalism and insurance premiums are higher in crowded urban centers.

In addition, because the school-age population in cities is diverse, urban school districts have usually offered more varied educational programs. Thus parents whose children have physical or mental handicaps tend to move to cities in order to gain access to special classes and teachers. Urban school districts have the additional responsibility of educating the culturally deprived and many students whose native language is not English; the local district must, therefore, support the costs of providing education geared specifically to these children. In general, special education is expensive education. If tne state does not provide additional support to meet particular needs, some students will again be penalized just because of where they live—the very result our proposed finance system seeks to avoid.

The kinds of categorical programs a school district might offer vary widely depending on location and characteristics of the school population. The most widespread categorical need is for compensatory education. Because this need is so compelling, we will discuss it at length in Chapter 4. Other categoricals we will mention here are construction, transportation, school lunch (and breakfast), and size-correction aid.

We have already shown that future construction can be fully funded by the state rather than be included in a local district's basic educational expenditure. In this way, the state would fund (with local approval) construction of a building, and the locality could fund additions or improvements from funds raised locally. The concept of state aid for the full cost of an adequate program and local expenditure for extras can be expanded to other areas of categorical need. Districts and the state must work closely together, of course, to determine a workable definition of an adequate program or building.

In many states local districts are already reimbursed for part of their transportation costs. Reimbursement is based either upon a formula (for instance, using sparsity as the factor to determine cost) or actual cost up to some fixed dollar limit. We hope that this program is expanded to cover the complete cost of transporting children to and from school. Formulas based upon sparsity, road conditions, weather conditions, and so on, can be devised to provide adequate funds for all districts without giving any district a blank check as would happen if full costs were reimbursed.

Other areas of categorical need include meals for needy children (presently federal aid partially pays for this program), the special costs of educating handicapped and gifted children, and costs generated by urban living (for insurance premiums, for example, or additional personnel hired to keep order). Preschool and after-school centers, both important parts of a district's program, can be either funded at cost or be included in a district's basic costs.

Additional costs of maintaining small schools should also be borne by the state, not the locality. One way to do this is to give extra weight to each student in a "necessarily small" school below a specific size. Alternatively, funds can be allocated on a per-classroom basis. A new bill in Kansas provides approximately 1¼ times (actually 1.285 times) as much money for each student in a district having less than 400 students as it does for each student in a district having over 1,300 students. Although the Kansas bill is a step in the right direction, it still does not cover the situation of small schools in large districts. Furthermore, all districts having more than 1,300 children are treated alike under this bill. But a district with only 1,300 students will find it more difficult to offer a varied high school program and keep classes filled than a district having, say, 25,000 students. Necessarily small schools should exist only when sparsity factors require them and not simply to perpetuate exclusive public schools for small pockets of wealthy families as is now often the case.

In Chapter 4 we will examine the possible negative effects of FSA and DPE on the poor and outline a number of safeguards that must be included in any finance plan to ensure that reform and reformers do not actually hurt those they are trying to help.

Problems of Implementation

Some problems must be considered before either FSA or DPE is implemented. First, any reform plan must consider the problem of cost differentials, especially in relation to teachers' salaries. The state may determine that there should be one teacher for every twenty-five pupils, but some teachers cost more to hire than others. Cost-of-living differentials among localities can be incorporated into state-aid formulas, but they will not cover all the variation in salaries. Some districts have been paying high salaries over many years in order to attract the best teachers; others might want to attract good teachers in this way but lack the financial resources to do so.

Some differentials are noneconomic and are therefore, more difficult to resolve. Clearly, most teachers, like most other people, would like to live in pleasant surroundings. Some schools, though, are located in isolated communities or in areas having uncomfortable climates. Even though housing costs may be lower in these districts than in more desirable areas, teachers will probably be attracted to them only if salary levels are relatively high. Thus such districts will likely be forced to offer high salaries to attract *any* teachers, not only the very best.

Second, these finance plans strive to equalize the ability of districts to raise money for current expenditures (salaries, supplies, pension funds, and so on) but do not equalize facilities from district to district. Given existing conditions, some districts will be housing students in mediocre buildings for some time while other districts will be able to educate their children in fully equipped classrooms. Obviously, these differences cannot be eradicated overnight. The state, however, can ensure that succeeding generations of children are educated in well-built, fully equipped schools.

There seems to be little justification for requiring a district to pay for its own school facilities. At present a rapidly growing district must heavily indenture itself in order to provide space for an expanding population; another district with a more stable school-age population may only have to replace its buildings as they become obsolete. We believe that the state should pay the full cost of a basic facility, with the stipulation that districts pay for all the extras such as swimming pools, additional laboratories, or music rooms. Each district's share of these extras would come out of its flat grant under FSA or its wealth-equalized grant under DPE. In addition to different building needs in different districts, land values and building costs vary enormously among districts, especially between urban and rural localities. A totally district-financed building program would place an excessive financial burden on urban districts where land costs are astronomical.

As a further complication, citizens may rightfully ask: Why should school districts that have already paid for their school buildings now have to help districts that are still repaying bonds? Moreover, why should districts that purchased minimal facilities assist those that bought lavish ones? And why should poor districts have to struggle to repay bonds that rich districts could easily repay? There are no simple answers to these questions. The easiest way to avoid the problem is to wait the thirty years for all bonds to be repaid. Alternatively, the state could undertake a major research effort to go through old blueprints, determine how much of the cost of each completed school building would have been approved for state financing, and then pay the amount of the current debt related to the appropriate costs. Under this scheme the district would pay the remainder of the debt. This method would be very expensive and time-consuming; it would probably cause much bitterness among districts and between districts and the state. A quicker solution would be to assume, based upon a district's wealth, that some fraction of its buildings would have been approved for state financing. Since this would hit rich districts hardest, it is not a politically attractive alternative. The problem of financing existing debts is certainly a sticky one; it must be resolved before any new finance scheme is implemented.

One last problem must be mentioned—under any equalizing scheme some cheating is bound to occur. A rich district may choose to locate its school library in an adjacent municipal library building and thereby ensure that the funds to support its library are additional to its general purpose grant. Under DPE a poor district may stretch the definition of education to the limit in order to get more subsidized dollars from the state. We recognize these possibilities and realize that some slight inequities will probably remain even after reform. We believe, though, that school finance reform can solve the gross inequities and allow for solution of other, less striking, inequities in the future.[5]

---

[5] Note that under DPE both rich and poor districts can cheat in the ways described; under FSA only the rich districts can cheat effectively. Also remember that under any financing system, the rich can "cheat" by providing their children with tutors, piano lessons, or dance classes.

Appendix to Chapter 3
District Power Equalizing Schedules
Further Examined

Many different kinds of DPE schedules have been proposed showing the relationship between expenditure and tax rate. Table 1, which we have already presented, outlines a DPE schedule in which there is a linear relationship between expenditure and tax rate. Figure 1a graphs this linear relationship. Figure 1b depicts a completely nonlinear schedule while Figure 1c shows a kinked linear schedule. Even discontinuous schedules as in Figure 1d have been proposed.

Our preference is for a kinked DPE schedule as shown in Figure 1c.[1] We advocate a minimum expenditure level, but for political reasons we believe it is necessary to keep the associated minimum tax rate low. With a kinked schedule it is possible to provide incentives (that is subsidies) to most districts (all but the richest) to spend above this minimum level. Obviously, such high subsidies could not be guaranteed at all expenditure levels because the state would risk bankruptcy by pouring money into local districts. The state can avoid this problem by altering the DPE schedule at some specified expenditure level, say $900. Up to this point districts would receive $250 per pupil for each $.50 increase in the tax rate. Above $900, however, a district would receive only $100 for each $.50 increase in tax rate. The "kink point" then is the preferred spending level because most districts have incentives to raise their spending levels to this point and disincentives for spending more. Since pressure to keep tax rates low will place an effective lid on local expenditures, the problem of establishing a ceiling on expenditure levels will not generally arise under a kinked schedule.

Even though the local district does have the final say about its expenditure level under DPE, the state obviously can influence the district's choice by the schedule it chooses. The state must first answer a number of questions about setting the relationship between expenditure level and tax rate: Should a minimum level be established below which no district may spend? Should there be a maximum level established, or will local taxpayer pressure be sufficient to determine an appropriate maximum? Should the

---

[1] Benson et al., *Final Report to the Senate Select Committee on School District Finance*, Sacramento, June 1972.

Figure 1 Examples of DPE Schedules

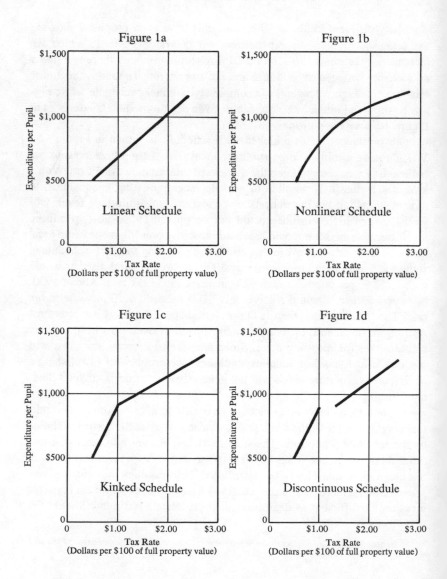

state encourage spending up to a point and no further by making it more expensive to increase expenditures (as in Figures 1c and 1d)? Whatever questions are asked, it is clear that the state cannot be neutral. It must first develop a schedule that will not bankrupt its treasury if many school districts vote for high expenditure levels.

The state cannot accurately predict the level of expenditure each district will choose. If poor districts vote for higher spending levels than rich districts, the state may lose money since it would have to provide more funds to supplement poor districts than it would recapture from rich districts. It may be, however, that rich people tend to value education more than poor people; since proportional taxation for education favors the rich, who have more disposable income, perhaps the rich would choose higher expenditures than the poor even under DPE.[2]

The state is not likely to be hurt financially if the DPE schedule is set near the average wealth per pupil in the state. There are ways for the state to act cautiously and guarantee that it will not spend more for education than it had originally intended. We will discuss this later when we explain how to phase-in a new system of finance.

From the point of view of a local district, a DPE schedule is quite different from the formulation of equal-wealth districts throughout the state. Under DPE, a very poor district may get $4 in state education aid for every $1 raised locally. Thus $1 in local revenue is worth $5 if spent on schools, but it is worth only $1 if spent on police, sewage, refuse collection, or libraries. On the other hand, a rich district may manage to keep only one-half of every dollar raised locally for schools while keeping all of every dollar raised and spent for other municipal services. (It is just this disincentive for rich districts and corresponding incentive for poor districts that leads Grubb and Feldstein to believe that poor districts will spend more than rich districts.) Consequently, DPE could distort the spending decisions of districts.

We must mention an important point here. Rich people have the option of sending their children to private schools. If the cost of maintaining a

---

[2] Experts disagree as to whether property rich districts (which may contain low-income people) will continue to spend more than poor districts. Under DPE, David Stern, "Effects of Alternative State Aid Formulas on the Distribution of Public School Expenditures in Massachusetts," *The Review of Economics and Statistics*, (LV, No. 1, February 1973: 91–97), predicts that spending will still be positively linked with wealth. Other experts such as Martin Feldstein of Harvard University and Norton Grubb of the University of California, Berkeley, take the opposite position for reasons explained below.

Figure 2 Phase-in Plan for a DPE Schedule

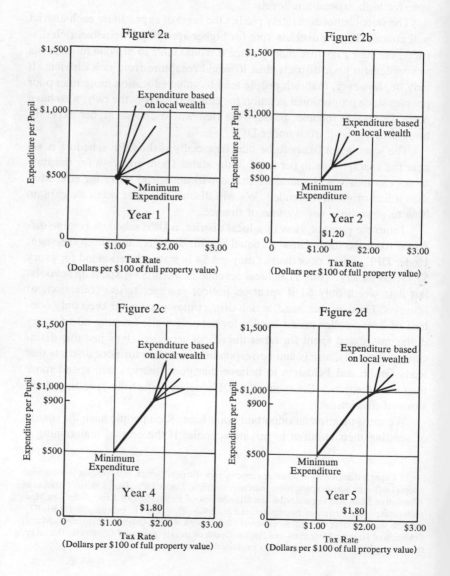

Figure 2e.   Completed Schedule

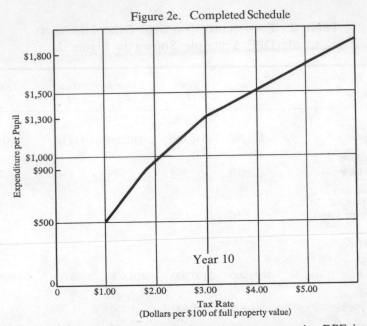

Tax Rate
(Dollars per $100 of full property value)

high level of spending in a public education system under DPE is sufficiently great, rich people in some districts might decide to abandon the
public sector. Mandating a minimum DPE expenditure level helps to prevent this by ensuring that the *additional* cost of providing a high-cost
public program will not be so great. Also, if many wealthy people in a district do decide to send their children to private schools, those others who do
not are guaranteed at least a minimal level of public support. It may be
true, furthermore, that people in a property rich district are somewhat
disinclined to appropriate money for education when they know that a
proportion of this money will not be spent in their district; there is a coun-
terbalancing desire on their part, however, not to forfeit the minimum expenditure level that they must support through state taxes whether or not
their children attend public schools. Obviously, this minimum must be sufficient to support a varied and interesting educational program. In any case,
if the state implements DPE, it has a stake—politically, economically, and
educationally—in keeping the rich within the public education system.

Figure 2 shows how a gradual DPE phase-in plan might look. In the
first year all districts would receive a grant of $500 per pupil paid for by a
property tax of $1 per $100 of full value and by new statewide taxes. Expenditures above this level would be supported by local wealth. In the sec-

Table 2 Possible Response of School Districts to the DPE Schedule Shown in Figure 2

District A	Year 0	Year 1	Year 2	Year 5	Year 10
Wealth per pupil	$10,000	$10,000	$10,000	$10,000	$10,000
Expenditure per pupil	600	650	710	1,000	1,000
Tax rate (per $100 of full property value)	3.00	2.50	2.30	2.10	2.10
District B					
Wealth per pupil	$100,000	$100,000	$100,000	$100,000	$100,000
Expenditure per pupil	1,500	1,400	1,350	1,300	1,150
Tax rate	1.50	1.90	1.95	2.30	2.55

ond year expenditures between $500 and $600 per pupil would be financed locally on a wealth-equalized basis in which $.20 of additional local tax rate generates the additional $100 per pupil. Spending above $600 in this second year would be based upon local wealth. A state can proceed in this way year by year, extending the wealth-equalized schedule by $100 (or any other value) each year.

Suppose after four years the state found itself subsidizing local district expenditures too much. In the fifth year it could then require, say, $.30 of additional tax instead of $.20 for a district to receive the next $100 as shown in Figure 2d. This change would discourage increased spending and also allow the state to recapture more money from richer districts. Figure 2e shows a completed DPE schedule after ten years.

The effects of such a phased-in DPE schedule would be this. Districts with low wealth in the first year would feel the effects of their new wealth gradually; thus they would slowly be able to raise their expenditures or lower their tax rate or do both. On the other hand, formerly high-wealth districts would gradually see their wealth position lowered; they would accordingly raise their tax rates or lower their expenditures or do both. Table 2 shows what may happen over time to one rich school district and one poor school district. (This example assumes that prior to adoption of the DPE plan the state's foundation plan guaranteed $400 per pupil with a district tax rate of $1 per $100 of full value.)

4

PROTECTING THE POOR
FROM REFORM

At a summer 1973 meeting of the Summer Economics Institute for Law Professors, one participant cited evidence suggesting the growing sophistication of economic analysis. Quoting findings published in 1965 by University of Chicago economist George Stigler, he noted that the proportion of articles published in leading American economic journals involving algebra, calculus, or geometry increased from 5 percent in 1892–93 to over 66 percent by 1962–63. The proportion using calculus increased from a negligible figure before 1922 to 46 percent in 1962–63. Undoubtedly, the tools available to economists and other social scientists are more numerous and sharply refined than ever before. Yet, despite the proliferation of social science research during the twentieth century, the disciplines of economics, politics, sociology, and psychology retain many subjective aspects. Social policy, relying heavily on the insights and findings of social science, rarely if ever is grounded in concrete scientific evidence. Social systems are exceedingly complex and are composed of infinite numbers of intricate relationships. They often defy the powers of the social scientist to explain and predict.

The 1960s produced a rash of social policy reform that included a war on poverty and crime, the construction of model cities, cleansing of the nation's fouled air and water resources, and promotion of "maximum feasible participation" of the poor in community programming. In support of this aggressive attack on the nation's ills, social science contributed a dazzling array of planning tools—systems analysis, Planning, Programming, and Budgeting Systems (PPBS), social indicators, decision theory, optimization modeling, computer assisted data retrieval, and operations research. Under the guise of science, which so successfully propelled Americans to the moon, policy planners sought to understand and tame the problems confronting Americans on this planet. But even as Neil Armstrong incredulously descended from the *Eagle* to place the first human foot on the moon, the giant step of man and science in space seemed piteously small to many on earth. The thrust to the moon and the efforts to ease America's social woes had begun at approximately the same time, and the crowning success of one only seemed to highlight the failure of the other. In August 1969 millions of Americans suffered from malnutrition; drug addiction was moving from the ghetto into the suburban middle class; city streets were more dangerous than ever; fish choked in the streams and people choked in the smog of Los Angeles, Gary, Pittsburgh, and Newark; and the outrage of the poor and the young at their political impotence was reaching its highest fervor. "If we could send man to the moon, why couldn't we . . . ?" became a frequent frustrating question. Dozens of irrelevant explanations were offered. The cynic pointed to corruption, incompetence, and deceit. The few optimists blamed insufficient funds, inadequate participation of groups affected by programs and policies and bureaucratic intransigence. Only a few people asked if social science and policy planners could really accomplish what people expected of them.

Today, Americans may be more sanguine about the possibilities of applying science to solving social problems. As Melvin Webber and Horst Rittel write:

A great many barriers are keeping us from perfecting a planning/governing system: theory is inadequate for decent forecasting; our intelligence is insufficient to our tasks; plurality of objectives held by pluralities of politics make it impossible to pursue unitary aims; and so on. The difficulties attached to rationality are tenacious, and we have so far been unable to get untangled from their web. This is partly because the classical paradigm of science and engineering—the paradigm that has underlain modern professionalism—is not applicable to the problems of open societal systems. One reason the public has been attacking the social professions, we believe, is that the cognitive and occupational styles of the professions—mimicking the cognitive style of science and the occupational style of engineering—have just not worked on a wide array of social problems . . . the social professions were misled somewhere along the line into assuming they could be applied scientists—that they could solve problems in the ways scientists can solve their problems. The error has been a serious one.[1]

Perhaps all of us find some solace in the inadequacies of social science. None of us wishes to see the spontaneity of our actions reduced to behavioral certainties spewed out by a formula programmed into a computer. There is a certain perversity in the prospect that our daily lives could become as predictable as the outcome of a chemical reaction.

If we successfully elude the probing of the social scientist, however, we must pay the price of misinterpretation and error in policy reform. It is the poor especially who are least able to afford the costs of reform. Consequently, they are also subjected to the highest risks. The failure of the war on poverty, for example, was not without cost for middle-class Americans, but it was largely devoid of risk for this group. The attack on poverty did not attempt to change the life style of middle-class America (although, if successful, it probably would have), only the life style of the poor. For the poor, however, the risks were high—bitter disappointment, alienation, and distrust resulted when the anticipated change failed to materialize.

This chapter explores methods of protecting the poor against failure in school reform. We must insist that our concern for the poor is not mired in the liberal paternalism that muddies so many reform efforts. Our comments are not directed mainly to poor people. The major problem in social policy reform is not saving poor people from themselves but from reformers. What we propose is not a method to guarantee the success of reform proposals but rather to ensure against their failure. The distinction is neither semantic nor trivial. The effects of reform usually matter greatly to those people who are touched by it. And the reformer cannot guarantee a correct reform. In many instances he will propose the wrong reform. Just as society does not hold the physician responsible for outcomes arising from unforeseen complications or the lack of developed medical procedures, it is unreasonable to penalize the reformer for what he does not and cannot yet know. He should be expected, however, to include with his proposals ways of compensating for undesirable side effects. Consequently, we will examine policies designed to avoid the foreseeable pitfalls.

As the courts began to affirm the logic set forth by school finance reformers in *Serrano* and other school finance litigation, the decisions were

---

[1] Horst W. J. Rittel ane Melvin M. Webber, "Dilemmas in a General Theory of Planning," Working Paper No. 194, Institute of Urban and Regional Development (Berkeley: University of California, November 1972).

hailed as revolutionary milestones that at last would help sever the tie between wealth and educational opportunity, easing the gross inequalities in educational spending that the existing system had produced. The courts took special notice of the relationship between the local tax base and educational spending. They expressed dismay at the ability of wealthier districts to spend large per-pupil amounts with small tax rates, or low tax efforts. Obviously, a child living in a property-poor district was less likely to receive the level of educational resources available to children in wealthier districts. Athough the courts did not outline a specific remedy for this problem, they very clearly stated that corrective measures must ensure that educational spending would not be a function of local wealth. They implied that while levels of spending need not be equal—they could differ according to rational educational criteria or even the preferences of consumers—equal per-pupil expenditures must be supported by equal tax rates. Either DPE or FSA satisfies these criteria.

On the surface the decision seems fair, and DPE and FSA appear to be workable solutions. Yet such efforts to ameliorate onerous fiscal burdens on poor school *districts* could have the effect of increasing the financial problems of poor families. This rather unusual result is easily accounted for. The California court, which boldly set the pattern of current reform efforts, chose the *school district* as the unit of analysis. The court found it distressing that poor school districts had to accept the burden of high local tax rates for schools even to maintain cheap (and presumably low quality) programs for their students; rich school districts, on the other hand, could enjoy the double advantage of low tax rates and lavish educational offerings. Reform efforts seek to achieve balance by improving the fiscal position of poor districts at the expense of rich districts. Poor families, then, receive benefits from educational reform if they live in poor districts. But poor families do not always live in poor districts.

This matter has been cogently discussed by Paul Dimond, staff attorney, Center for Law and Education, Harvard University. In Dimond's view the "real financial issue in American education has to do with poor children, not poor districts." Indeed, he says, "the equal protection clause [of the Fourteenth Amendment] speaks to the rights of *individuals,* not *districts.*" Yet by concentrating on districts the courts have picked a weapon (to help the poor) that is extremely unwieldy. Dimond notes further: "To give . . . the most obvious example, in New York State clearly New York City is one of the richest school districts, yet it has by far the largest percentage and number of poor children. So that for New York State it simply is not true that poverty of children is related directly to poverty of districts, for the poor children are in one of the richest districts." [2] Similarly, the San Francisco Unified School District, which enrolls 80,000 students, is a very rich district. Yet 24 percent of San Francisco families earn less than $6,000 per year, and 10 percent of all families (representing 13.6 percent of the population) fall below the poverty level.

Some poor people do, of course, live in poor districts. Cities in New Jersey, such as Newark, that have low property values also have many poor residents. So do many older industrial towns in New England. Many districts in the South are property-poor and also populated by people with low incomes. The cities and towns of the great agricultural valleys in California have concentrations of household poverty, and frequently they are poor in local taxables as well. The point is simply that poor people live in all types of districts, as characterized by assessed valuation per student. Hence, reform policies that attack interdistrict inequities too simply are bound to do financial damage to about as many poor families as they help.

Certain reform proposals might yield such a result. In 1972 the New York State Fleischmann Commission recommended full state assumption of educational funding. It also recommended several hundred other actions, the majority of which would have offered benefits to poor households. Here we will consider the effects of the full state funding recommendation *as if* the legislature in New York had accepted the full state funding recommendation and none other. In 1970–71, 21 districts out of a total 750 enrolled 12,500 students or more—roughly 1,000 per grade. The proposed statewide school property tax rate (substitution of state for local property taxation is an integral feature of FSA recommendations) would have required New York City, Buffalo, Rochester, Syracuse, and Yonkers—the "big five" cities—to *increase* the contribution demanded of their property owners (and, one may assume, of renters) to support schools. All but six of the remaining large districts would have received

    [2] Paul Dimond, "The Judicial Impact," in Federal Reserve Bank of Boston, *Financing Public Schools* (Boston: The Bank, 1972), pp. 61, 63, 65. Along the same line it is interesting to note that a study of education finance in California simulated the effects of a sophisticated DPE proposal on the owners of the lowest quartile (by assessed valuation) of owner-occupied homes (assessed value less than $4,376) in an eight-county sample of the state. The conclusion was: "Nearly half of these low-wealth households [would] experience an increase in school tax rates. About 14 percent of them would suffer property rate increases greater than $2.50 per $100 of assessed value (statewide average school rate before the increase being roughly $5.00)." See Charles S. Benson et al., *Final Report to the Senate Select Committee on School District Finance*, 2 vols. (Sacramento, Cal.: The Committee, 1972), p. 83.

reductions in property taxes for schools, and they include such middle-class Long Island communities as East Meadow, Levittown, Massapequa, Commack, Brentwood, and Smithtown. Now, the "big five" cities include the majority of poor households in all of New York State. The six Long Island communities, on the other hand, are definitely middle class. Thus the full state funding recommendation, if taken alone, would pit the poor in a losing position, against the middle class. It is not surprising, then, that poor households apparently have not taken much interest in the new orthodoxy of school reform.

Another approach to reform is to combine a recommendation for FSA with a proposal for massive reduction in property taxes. Because property taxes are frequently regarded as particularly burdensome on poor households, this might appear to be an egalitarian thing to do. In California the Watson Amendment was a plan for a state takeover of school finance with property tax reduction. The amendment failed to gain voter approval in 1972. But it is interesting to note what might have happened in two contrasting and neighboring towns in the San Francisco Bay region—Piedmont, an area of rich households, and Emeryville a town of poor households—had the Watson Amendment been passed. On the basis of 1970–71 data Piedmont's school tax rate would have dropped from $5.17 per $100 of assessed valuation to $2.20, a reduction of $2.97. Of 3,641 single-family residences in Piedmont, 1,161 have assessed valuation in excess of $12,500 (that is, one-fourth of a market value of $50,000). Ninety-two percent of these houses are occupied by owners. Occupants of these dwellings typically have annual incomes in excess of $35,000. For the 1,161 residences with assessed values of $12,500, the school tax savings generated by the Watson Amendment would amount to $640,505—yielding an average of $552 per house.

In Emeryville 209 of the 221 single-family residences have assessed valuations of less than $6,500 (the market value being $26,000). Only 49 percent of these houses are owner-occupied. Typical annual income in an Emeryville household is less than $15,000. Yet, because Emeryville has a great deal of industrial property, it has a low tax rate. Accordingly, Emeryville's school tax rate reduction under the Watson formula would be modest—$.44 (down from $2.66 to $2.22). School tax savings on the residential properties valued at less than $6,500 amount to only $3,537—an average of $17 per residence.

Thus, in the case at hand, the proposal aimed at massive reduction in local property tax burdens for schools benefits rich households much more than poor ones. Piedmont's average saving per house of market value $50,000 and over would equal $46 per month; Emeryville's average saving per house of market value under $26,000 would equal only $1.42 a month. To some extent this contrast is moderated by the fact that Piedmont residents generally itemize deductions on personal income tax returns; thus a fall in property tax is partly offset by an increase in tax liability. But the advantage to rich households is not completely washed away by this fact.

The third example of a reform proposal that is likely to penalize the poor grows naturally out of the second. It has been suggested that the state take over the taxation of nonresidential properties. Currently, the power of localities to tax factories, shopping centers, hotels, public utilities, and so on, is chiefly responsible for the very wide differences among districts in taxing capacity. These wide differences produce, in turn, an educational system that is chaotic and unjust. Why not attack the specific cause of the irregularity, then, and give the state government the exclusive power to make levies on nonresidential assets?

If this were the case, however, the principal losers would be poor households, not the owners of the income-producing properties. The latter, after all, have the means to pass along to the consumer at least a portion of any increase in taxes they might have to pay, and some owners of capital—that is, capital situated in low-wealth districts—would actually enjoy reductions in their tax bill. But for poor families who desire to enjoy expensive public services, there are only two options. One is to move into an industrial tax haven and accept the grime, smoke, noise, and congestion that characterize such areas in exchange for high-priced public services supported by the expanded tax base. The second option is to move into a low-income neighborhood of a large city. Large cities, after all, have a very diversified local tax base, and ordinarily they offer high-expenditure public services to their residents. Removing nonresidential property from local taxation could wipe out both of these options.

It does indeed seem peculiar that the apparently clear and just Proposition I of the *Serrano* doctrine can lay additional financial burdens on the poor, even when they live in a small governmental unit, such as Emeryville. This fact points out a weakness in the fiscal policy of state governments. In the early 1800s property or capital was rather closely attached to its owner in a physical sense. A wealthy man usually possessed arable land, water, farm buildings, agricultural equipment, income-producing animals—and his house. A poor man might have some of these same things, though in much smaller quantity, or he might be landless and bereft of property altogether. This description of the distinction between wealth and poverty is still an accurate one for the majority of the people who live in the developing world. As long as it properly describes the wealth situation in a given country, the *Serrano* doctrine is almost certain to lead directly toward equitable reforms.

In the United States and the rest of the developed, nonsocialist world, there is no longer the close physical connection between wealth and residence. If a person is a very large shareholder in a firm, he may never even see the physical assets of the enterprise, for they may be located in an out-of-the-way area. Once owners of property realized that they no longer needed to live on the farm or down the street from the mill, they saw that it was possible to reduce their tax bills as well. The trick was to have state officials draw local boundaries so as to maximize the concentration of capital and minimize the number of residents who desire expensive public services. In California, for example, the school districts of Buena Vista and Elk Hills in Kern County, an oil rich region, have, respectively, 40 and 90 students. They both register assessed valuations per elementary student in excess of $300,000. Bakersfield, the largest city in Kern County, has over 23,000 elementary students but only $8,300 of assessed valuation per student to tax for their schooling. When tax havens are created, properties are granted legal means to avoid paying taxes. Tax havens should be abolished but in such a way that neither the education nor the financial position of poor families is placed at risk.

A First Step: Income-Specific Property Tax Relief

Clearly the basic reforms implied by the courts must be modified if poor households are to benefit from school finance reform. One method, now used by a few states to protect their senior citizens (and in Oregon all citizens regardless of age) from onerous property tax burdens is the circuit breaker.

A circuit breaker guarantees that a lower-income household will pay no more than a specified portion of its annual income in property taxes, regardless of the actual property tax rate in effect and the value of the household's property. In its simplest form, for example, a circuit breaker may provide that a household earning less than $10,000 per year will pay no more than 5 percent of its annual income in property tax. Consider a family that owns a house valued at $15,000. Assume that the family income is

$5,000 per year and the community tax rate is $3 per $100 of full value (3 percent). Without a circuit breaker this family would pay $450 in property taxes. A circuit breaker specifying a limit of 5 percent of annual income, however, would reduce this family's property tax liability to $250. The additional $200 would be returned to the family by the state (as in the case of income tax refunds); if the family had paid only $250, the $200 would be paid to the municipality by the state. In either case the local community would receive the full $450. Note that in this example a family earning $5,000 is not affected by increases in the tax rate beyond $1.67 per $100 of assessed valuation (a $1.67 tax rate produces $250 of property tax on a $15,000 house). Any increase is paid by the state. Consequently, if this family lives in a wealthy school district having a low tax rate, it will not be significantly harmed by tax increases required by a DPE scheme.

Under FSA part or all of the cost of the program can be funded by nonproperty taxes. But if FSA is funded primarily by property taxes, the poor in property rich districts would experience property tax rate increases just as under DPE. Thus while the circuit breaker primarily prevents problems when a DPE plan is implemented, it may also be necessary in a FSA scheme. We also want to note here that if FSA is funded largely by nonproperty taxes, these taxes should be progressive so that the poor do not suffer from large tax increases.

A more sophisticated version of the circuit breaker is one that provides a progressive scale of relief. A family earning less than $2,000, for example, might be responsible for no more than 1 percent of its income in property taxes; families earning between $2,000 and $4,000, no more than 2 percent; families earning between $4,000 and $6,000, no more than 3 percent; and so on. Alternatively, the state might pay a specified portion of a family's property tax bill, depending on the family's income—96 percent of the bill if the family earned less than $1,000; 80 percent if between $2,500 and $3,000; 45 percent if between $4,500 and $5,000; and so on, to perhaps 4 percent if between $9,500 and $10,000.[3]

This last method for calculating property tax relief has a distinct advantage over the other proposals that provide no additional tax payment if the tax rate exceeds some levy (such as $1.67 in our earlier example). When people pay a percentage of every tax dollar levied under this plan, the disincentive to choose high tax rates is preserved. With DPE especially, this

---

[3] This method is currently used in California for senior-citizen relief, and an expanded version was recommended by the Consultant Staff in Benson et al., *Final Report to the Senate Select Committee on School District Finance*.

disincentive is necessary to keep the spending of low-income districts in line with that of high-income districts.

Thus the circuit breaker is necessary to protect the poor from property tax increases required by school finance reform. The device is not without its problems, however. First, there is the problem of adequately defining "income." In states where a circuit breaker is presently in use, income is defined as adjusted gross income as computed for income tax procedures. This procedure permits ease in computing circuit-breaker relief, since claims may be verified against federal or state income tax returns. Its major disadvantage is that some income (for example, income from tax-free municipal bonds) need not be reported for tax purposes. Individuals with substantial incomes from such sources might therefore be able to claim property tax relief if income from taxable sources is within the limits of the circuit breaker. Such individuals, however, are probably few in number; moreover the costs of identifying them and preventing their claiming relief would probably exceed any money to be saved by the state once they had been found.

A related but more serious problem arises for welfare recipients claiming relief under such a proposal. Federal regulations require welfare payments to be reduced by an amount equivalent to cash income received. Direct application of the circuit breaker to welfare recipients therefore would have the effect of merely replacing rather than supplementing welfare payments. A solution to this problem is to direct individual relief to welfare offices with the stipulation that it be added to the individual's shelter allowance for "unmet shelter needs."

Finally, there is the problem of whether to include renters under the protection of the circuit breaker. If so, how should they be included? Renters, of course, do not pay property taxes directly. Whether property taxes are included in rents and therefore paid indirectly by renters is a matter of some debate among economists. There is nearly unanimous agreement, however, that the tax on the value of land alone is paid by landowners. That is, when the property tax is initially levied, or when it is increased, the net income from land is reduced by the amount of the tax. As a result, the value of the land falls, sometimes substantially. Consider a piece of farm land yielding a net income of $10,000 per year. Assume that you are an investor who expects a 10-percent return on money that you invest in this farmland. You base your 10-percent requirement on the knowledge that you could obtain a *guaranteed* 6-to-7 percent return by simply placing your funds in a long-term savings account. Since farming involves some risk—poor weather, plant diseases, fluctuations in food prices, and so on—you set your expected return at 10 percent. Since this particular farm yields a net income of $10,000, the value of the land is $100,000. But before you enter an agreement to buy the farm, the local school district levies a 1-percent property tax, amounting to $1,000 per year on this farm. Net income is reduced to $9,000. Your requirement for a 10-percent rate of return has not changed, however. Now you are willing to pay only $90,000 for the land, since this is the amount that will yield a 10-percent return. A 1-percent tax, collecting $1,000 per year on this farm, has reduced the value of the farm by $10,000.

This decrease in the value of the land, called capitalization in economics, produces a curious result. The original landowner, that is, the owner when the tax is imposed, absorbs the *full* impact of the property tax. The supply of land is fixed, so he cannot get a price better than $90,000 for his land. If he agrees to sell the land to you, he must sell it at $90,000. In buying it, however, you will not really pay the property tax. You will of course send in the check to the local school district, but unless the rate is increased, the tax is of no concern to you. You paid $90,000 for the farm, are receiving $9,000 in net income, and therefore are obtaining the 10-percent return you expected. In other words, if you buy land after the tax is imposed and if the tax rate is not increased, theoretically you do not bear the cost of the property tax even though you continue to send in a check for the tax forever! The tax is paid by the decrease in land value, a capital loss that falls entirely on the owner when the tax is imposed.

What remains uncertain is who pays the property tax on structures and improvements. To what extent do the owners of apartment buildings shift the burden of property taxation by raising rents? In the case of owner-occupied houses, it is clear that owners pay the property tax, since they are also the consumers and could shift the tax only to themselves. Hence, there is strong economic justification for a circuit breaker protecting lower-income homeowners from increases in property tax rates. But is there justification for protecting renters? The question is particularly important in regard to low-income families, who are more likely to rent housing than own it.

On this question, there are two divergent opinions. Both groups begin by recognizing that unlike land, the supply of housing is not fixed. (We should probably say that the supply of housing is less fixed. Land can be created through drainage and fill, or arid land can be made productive through irrigation. In relative terms, however, the point still holds.) One group maintains that since property taxes reduce the rate of return to owners of rental housing, the lower rate of return dampens investors' interest in building housing. As building slows—that is, as the supply of housing decreases—prices go up until the old rate of return has been restored. Therefore, since renters pay higher prices, they also pay the tax.

The other group holds that when the rate of return falls in rental housing, investors turn their attention to other more lightly taxed areas of the economy. The supply of housing still diminishes, and rental prices rise; but the supply of other goods increases, and their prices fall. (Or, alternatively, given inflation and our lack of experience with falling prices, prices of other goods do not rise as quickly.) As prices of these other goods fall, the rate of return is reduced until a lower rate of return prevails throughout the economy. Consumers as a group do not lose, since higher housing rents are offset by lower prices elsewhere. Rather the tax is borne by owners of capital who now receive a lower return on their investment. Even under this second argument there is reason for concern. If investment moves from capital-intensive industries (such as housing and agriculture) into more lightly taxed industries (labor-intensive services, such as entertainment, medicine, law) consumers who devote larger portions of their incomes to purchases of food and housing will lose, while those who devote smaller portions will gain. Clearly, lower-income families fall into the first consumer group. *Thus there is strong economic justification for protecting low-income renters from property tax increases.* Including renters in a circuit-breaker scheme, however, does present some difficulties.

Foremost is the problem of determining what portion of rent represents property taxes. Again economic analysis cannot provide any precise estimate. In California the staff of the state committee investigating school district finance in 1972 assumed that property taxes averaged 20 percent of gross rent. Since for families with incomes below $10,000, gross rent is on the average about 25 percent of income, it follows that property taxes are about 5 percent of family income. But allowing all renters to claim property taxes equal to 5 percent of income would overstate the tax paid by many renters. Therefore, it seems preferable to make instead a standard allowance of 4 percent, without requiring renters to submit any evidence of actual rent paid. A family that actually does pay more than 20 percent of its income for rent could claim property taxes equal to 20 percent of actual rent paid by submitting proof of the amount paid.

Renters who choose to claim property tax relief based on actual rent paid face some problems in defining what rent includes. Rent payments reflect different amounts of services provided by landlords—heat, water, refuse removal, furnishings, and so on. Water and refuse removal are included in most rental agreements and could arbitrarily be assumed to be included in all rental payments. To avoid overreimbursing tenants who receive additional services, standard percentage deductions from gross rent could be made for each of the following: heat, gas or electricity, pool, sauna, garage, and furnishings.

A renter claiming relief would simply submit regular income statements, noting whether he chooses to count imputed property taxes as 4 percent of income or 20 percent of actual rent paid. Unrelated individuals sharing rental units would be required to submit income statements listing each member's income on the relief claim. Once imputed property taxes had been calculated for renters, the same relief measure would apply for renters and homeowners. The state would calculate each claimant's relief, credit this relief against state income tax liability (if any), and refund any excess to the claimant.

A circuit breaker, therefore, offers a sensible method for providing property tax relief. It focuses relief on individual households for whom the tax burden is onerous. It has the added advantage of alleviating the additional tax burden on low-income families that live in school districts in which assessed value and expenditures per pupil are high and in which tax rates must increase after the introduction of DPE. Thus it is an essential mechanism if the poor are to benefit financially from school finance reform.

Income-Based Grants: An Alternative to the Circuit Breaker

One major difficulty posed by the circuit breaker is that it is not part of the fundamental formula for distributing educational funds. Legislatures may ignore it completely in enacting a reform plan. Consequently, there is some interest in building protection into the distribution formula itself. One way is to create a progressive DPE schedule reflecting a district's distribution of household income. Progressive DPE would require less tax effort in districts with relatively lower amounts of household income per pupil. Suppose, for example, that on the average the DPE schedule provides an additional $100 per pupil for a $1 increase in the local tax rate. Assume that for the state, as a whole, average household income is $8,000 per pupil. In a district having only $6,000 of household income per pupil (75 percent of the state average), the required additional rate, under progressive DPE, would be only $.75. In a district having $10,000 of household income per pupil (125 percent of the state average) the tax rate would be $1.25. In other words, the DPE rate for each district would be multiplied by the ratio of the district's household income per pupil to the state average household income per pupil. In terms of a formula:

$$\text{Actual Tax Rate} = \text{DPE Tax Rate} \times \frac{\text{District Household Income per Student}}{\text{State Household Income per Student}}$$

Such a formula would reduce the tax rate for all districts having high concentrations of low-income families, including those districts with large amounts of assessed valuation. Moreover, unlike the circuit breaker, it has the advantage of capturing and equalizing the benefits accruing to districts having more high-income households.

Nevertheless, progressive DPE contains several flaws. It protects districts rather than individuals. Consequently, in a city like San Francisco, where there are concentrations of both low- and high-income families, the income effects are averaged out. The poor are overtaxed; the rich undertaxed. In industrial enclaves the presence of poor families reduces the general property tax rate, protecting not only poor families but also the owners of commercial and industrial property who may not deserve such protection on ability-to-pay criteria. (A separate tax on nonresidential property would alleviate this last problem.) In comparison, the circuit breaker is more direct and offers greater assurance that lower income families will receive the protection they need.

Major Categorical Grants: Income and Achievement

Although income-based grants do not offer an attractive alternative to the circuit breaker, a strong argument can be made for *supplementing* a reform scheme and a circuit-breaker plan with income and achievement grants. Either DPE or FSA equalizes the fiscal capability of school districts; the circuit breaker protects low-income families from tax increases resulting from such equalization. But equalizing educational resources and fiscal tax burdens falls far short of ensuring equal educational opportunity for children from low-income families. These children enter school at a distinct disadvantage. They have not received the benefits of preschool preparation ordinarily purchased privately by the parents of wealthier children. Moreover, as a child's school life continues, wealthier parents continue to supplement privately the child's public school experience in a variety of ways—music, art, or dance instruction, summer camps, private tutoring, book clubs, and family travel, to name but a few. It is no surprise that the achievement gap between low- and high-income children widens as educational experience progresses. The situation has been viewed this way:

> The segregation of disadvantaged youths—disadvantaged financially, in their prospects, in the perceptions of the value of education, in their developed verbal and intellectual skills, in their interests—creates an encapsulated society with a distinctive sub-culture. Pupils reinforce each others' views of the world rather than challenging them by exposing diversity. The standards of success which bring esteem from one's peers are largely non-academic—but to the small extent that they are academic the norm is low. Teachers—especially teachers who have remained for a long period in such an enclosed milieu— normalize these same standards. Their expectations for performance are adapted to the levels with which they have been confronted. Particularly where group instruction is the common practice instead, the level of instruction is aimed where at least some fraction of the class can understand. Where substantial proportions of students are unmotivated, a larger fraction of class time is devoted to behavioral control than to instruction.[4]

Yet, if it is true that children from low-income families are educationally disadvantaged, it is certainly not true that all low-income children fail in school. Nor do all high-income children succeed. Although there exists a high correlation between school achievement and socioeconomic status, the relationship is not perfect. A continuing point of controversy is whether school funds should be distributed on the basis of low income or low achievement. Given the high inverse correlation between school success and social class, it might at first appear to make no difference. On the contrary, we feel the question is an important one, and we strongly suggest that both bases of distribution—social class and school success—be employed.

---

[4] Interestingly, this statement was written with respect to disadvantaged youth in Malaysia. The problem, we think, is worldwide. See Kuala Lumpur, *Study of Opinion About Education and Society* (Malaysia: Ministry of Education, 1973), p. 38.

In the first place, choosing a distribution mechanism implies a certain policy objective. Each of the two alternative forms of distribution implies a different and important objective. When low income level is the basis for distribution, the public policy goal is to help students from poor households reach their individual potentials. Some students from poor households may have undiagnosed—and, hence, untreated—medical problems. They may suffer from dietary deficiencies. They may be burdened with caring for siblings and sick parents—responsibilities unknown to many children in middle-class households. They may lack a quiet study area. Because of such difficulties, a very bright but very poor young student might make only an average score in achievement tests. The aim of income-based compensatory education grants is to make certain his talent is discovered by giving him the opportunity to develop his skills and score near the top in such tests. In this way, he might identify himself as a candidate for some specialized form of higher education. Necessarily, grants distributed on the basis of low income will be spread out over all low-income students, whether they succeed or fail in school.

It is often argued that the schools cannot be expected to solve problems produced by inadequate home and community environments. Children spend about six hours per day in school, and this amount of time is further reduced by school vacations, illnesses, and other absences. Teachers frequently complain that in-school accomplishments are too easily undone when children return to their out-of-school environments. Moreover, increasing attention to classroom social class and racial integration, a positive step, increases the possibility that additional resources will not reach the children for whom they are intended. We do not view this problem cynically. The vast majority of educators are indeed well-intentioned individuals who desire to see that resources reach the children who need them most. But as long as classrooms are integrated racially, socially, and economically, it is inevitable that resource "leakage" occurs. That is, too much money leaks to students who are doing well enough by ordinary standards. Reserving special classroom supplies or personnel for certain students is a difficult task and, given possible stigmatizing effects, quite possibly one that should not be encouraged.

It follows that income-based grants are not finely adjusted instruments for attacking the problem of school failure per se. Educational failure is a terrible problem. Not only is the individual's own life blighted, but his failure to learn in school may lead him as an adult into socially unacceptable patterns that are harmful to himself and others. In order to channel funds toward failing students, the grant-distribution scheme would have to be regulated by the incidence of failure in the different schools of a state. Grants distributed on the basis of low-achievement scores will direct some funds into affluent suburban districts, where incidences of school failure also occur. Since low-achievement grants spread money over all the income classes to some degree, they do not concentrate exclusively on poor youth, and they are not as effective as income-based grants in attacking the noxious association between poverty and the failure to allow one's potential—at whichever level that potential may exist—to be realized.[5]

Not only do the two alternative criteria imply different objectives, they also imply differences in the specific uses to which the funds should be put.

> Studies in educational production have indicated that inputs associated with both home and school environments are important determinants of student achievement. We suggest a natural partition of compensatory education funds along these lines. The portion of funds meant to provide low SES children with equal opportunity to develop their potential should be used to supplement those resources normally provided by the home and neighborhood environment. That portion of funds meant to improve the performance of low achievers should be used to provide special instructional personnel, programs, and facilities within the school for use of those students. Not only does our suggestion follow logically from the rationale for the two kinds of compensatory funds; it also suggests that it is best to target funds to low SES students through the community (for health, nutrition and recreational services, say) and funds to low achieving students through the school.[6]

In somewhat greater detail, income-based grants seeking to overcome the inadequacies of home and community might properly be spent to improve these environments. These grants, distributed through school-community agencies to low-income neighborhoods could be used to support a variety of programs. They could provide essential health care to preschool and school children, basic nutrition through a breakfast program, and pro-

---

[5] The details of a two-pronged compensatory education distribution scheme have been worked out in detail in Benson et al., *Final Report to the Senate Select Committee*, pp. 39–44 and are not repeated here. We simply note the summary paragraph about the proposed distribution (p. 40): "The amount of aid allocated to a district on behalf of any student would be determined by (1) the difference between the student's SES [socioeconomic status] and the mean for the state and (2) the difference between his grade one test score and the mean for the state. Furthermore, the larger these differences are, the higher is the amount of aid which is allocated to the student. Funds to the district as a whole would simply be the sum of the allocations for the individual students in the district."

[6] Benson et al., *Final Report to the Senate Select Committee*, p. 41.

fessional assistance to students outside of school. They might be used to support preschool day-care facilities with an emphasis on child care and opportunities for education within the home. The possibilities are endless; the central point is that such grants should focus on measures aimed at solving problems that occur in the home and neighborhood.

Achievement-based grants, on the other hand, should focus on what schools do best, providing professional instructional and counseling personnel. In our conversations with teachers and administrators, one of the most frequently voiced concerns is the lack of time or funds for in-service training. Most teachers and counselors simply do not have enough time to stay abreast of improvements in methodology, classroom technology, and teaching materials that would help them be more effective in their work. Many schools lack specialized personnel to identify learning handicaps of individual children or provide the necessary therapy for effective learning.

We now come to an important dilemma. We have continually stressed the desirability of social class integration. How are special resources to reach the intended student if integration effectively reduces the concentration of needy pupils in particular schools and classrooms? Let us sketch the problem at somewhat greater length. It is generally agreed among social psychologists that social class integration works best when it commences early in the life of a child—in pre-school, kindergarten, and primary grades. It is also generally agreed that integration is ineffective, if not positively harmful, unless it extends into the classroom itself. This means that classification of students by rate of learning—that is, tracking or streaming and other forms of stigmatizing young people—is counterproductive for the purposes of integration.

Federal guidelines allow Title I grants to "follow the child on the bus to his integrated school" but insist that the funds be concentrated on the target population. State compensatory education programs incorporate similar guidelines. Now, if integration takes place among very young students, if no distinctions readily detectable by children are to be made in their learning programs, and if compensatory funds are to be concentrated in the early years of school life, then it would seem that the conscientious school authority has no choice but to provide a highly enriched program for *all students* in their early years. But plainly this is an unrealistic though desirable notion. If effective programs for low achievers were put into operation in our large cities, to extend the financial equivalent of these programs to all students would put unnecessary strain on the already overburdened tax base of the cities. It would place special penalties on the very suburban districts that chose to participate in integration schemes. And it would not solve the problem of how to give different kinds of help to students in a primary classroom (clearly, slow learners and fast learners need different kinds of help) without labeling and stigmatizing students.

At its core, the dilemma probably cannot be adequately resolved. But the recognition and use of the twofold character of compensatory education funds and programs, mentioned previously, takes us a long way toward its resolution. In the first place, grants distributed on the basis of low income and used for home-support services (health care, nutrition, and the like) present no problem, because the money would be spent outside of school and would, therefore, establish no basis for stigma.

What of funds distributed on the basis of low achievement and used within a school setting? First, if the stand is taken that problems of low achievement exist in all classrooms—that even children from affluent homes fall into the low-achievement group in any given classroom—and that these problems are expected to be temporary, then educational stigma is clearly distinguished from class stigma. Secondly, if several adults were to work in a classroom at the same time, they could give individualized attention to all students so that stigma would be lessened or avoided. The same positive result would occur if adults purposefully avoided stigmatizing children. A third possibility is for districts and regional authorities to design and offer *voluntary* after-school and summer programs for very young children before they customarily enter formal education settings. Such programs should attempt to stimulate the child's curiosity and interest in learning and be planned to appeal to the child who may be expected to have learning difficulties as well as to the average child. The county, for instance, should expect to meet a proportion of the cost of these programs from its own resources. This might be roughly indicated by the proportion of children attending who are free of expected learning difficulties, but the level of expenditure should be within the capacity of almost all educational authorities.

We have already seen that *Serrano*-style reform can have the effect of reallocating educational resources toward the middle class—recall what would happen under FSA to the relative position of the large cities of New York State as compared with the middle-class suburbs of Long Island. It follows that reform could have the effect of widening the already shocking gap between the average school performance of middle-class and poor youth. It is not enough, then, to try to protect the poor from unfair consequences of educational reform in regard to taxes; it is also important to make certain that the quality of school programs for poor youth be raised. The cost of this will not be inconsequential. The Fleischmann Commission's recommendation that low-achieving students be counted with an extra weight for distribution purposes (1.5 as compared with 1.0 for an average student) would have increased urban education grants by the state of New York approximately seven times. In California the study staff of the Senate Select Committee proposed that the state should provide $500 million annually for this purpose, approximately six times as much as is presently laid out from state revenue sources.

The General Financial Problems of Large Cities

It is probably futile to seek to improve the lot of the urban poor—now by far the majority of American poor—through education-related devices alone. As long as cities are unsafe, unsanitary, and in a state of physical deterioration, they will repel the middle class and further encapsulate low-income families.

We venture to say that few Americans think too highly of the condition of our large cities or of the quality of life within them. When our cities are not dangerous, they are generally faceless and lacking in character. As reported in the *New York Times* in July 1973: "According to a 1972 [Gallup] poll, six of ten citizens believe [Mayor] Lindsay's government is working poorly; nine of 100 think it good. A separate survey tells us that 45 percent of New Yorkers think their neighborhoods have worsened in the last five years. Less than a sixth of that number think the place where they live is better now." [7] At the same time when Americans travel in Europe, they spend most of their time in cities and apparently enjoy being in cosmopolitan settings.

Many efforts, some quite imaginative, have already been made in an effort to improve the quality of urban life in America. We clearly do not pretend to offer a comprehensive set of solutions to problems facing large cities, though many such comprehensive plans are available, as any student in city planning can attest. What we discuss here, as in our other chapters, is reform of financial arrangements to support public services that affect the lives of young people.

[7] Jeff Greenfield, "Hail and Farewell: Reading John Lindsay's Face," *The New York Times Magazine*, 29 July 1973, p. 8.

In a study prepared for the New York State Fleischmann Commission, Harvey E. Brazer and his associates in the economics department of the University of Michigan were able to predict with reasonable accuracy the level of nonschool municipal expenditures in representative cities of New York State. "The approach used to arrive at these estimates of needs involves multiple regression analysis that enables us to derive estimating equations for expenditures on each of the major functional categories of non-school expenditure." [8] In the case of public safety, for instance, including expenditures for municipal police and fire service, jails, safety inspections, and so on, 76 percent of the differences in per-capita local expenditures in 104 jurisdictions of the state were explained by the following variables: crime rate, population density, proportion of local tax base represented by industrial and commercial holdings, proportion of old housing (structures built prior to 1940) in the locality, population growth, and fiscal capacity.[9] Seventy-three percent of interurban differences in expenditures on streets and highways are accounted for by the variables of geographic size, population density, proportion of industrial, commercial, and seasonal (for example, vacation homes) property in the tax base, and fiscal capacity.[10] Similar equations were developed to explain variation of expenditures among cities in all other important public programs.

In other words, requirements to spend are not randomly arranged in our local government. If one knows a few simple and readily available facts about a locality, one can easily figure how much is spent, per capita, for general government, public safety, streets and highways, sanitation, health services, amenities (such as libraries, museums, zoos, parks, extension services, community colleges, conservation), and welfare. This information can be put to important use, namely, to regulate general purpose grants (excluding lower education, which we feel is a matter to be treated separately) to its localities.

The basic mechanics of such a scheme would be as follows. Equations would be derived, as in Brazer's work, to predict expected local public expenditures (per capita); one or more equations would apply to each major service. For each locality that receives a grant, expenditure requirements in each major service would be estimated by substituting in the regression

[8] Harvey E. Brazer et al., "Fiscal Needs and Resources: A Report to the New York State Commission on the Quality, Cost and Financing of Elementary and Secondary Education" (New York: The Commission, 1971), pp. 5–10.

[9] Ibid., pp. 5–21.

[10] Ibid., pp. 5–23.

equations the actual values for the predicted variables—the locality's geographic size, density, socioeconomic characteristics of the population, characteristics of physical capital located within its boundaries (but probably excluding physical capacity), and so on. Its expected expenditures for all major nonschool services would then be added together. The resulting sum would be the "expenditure need." The revenue yield at the minimum nonschool local tax rate would then be subtracted from this estimate of expenditure need. (The minimum local tax rate might be uniform across a whole state or region, or it might be differentiated by average income level of households in the community.) Modern facilities for data analysis would allow this kind of grant calculation to be made easily for the largest 5,000 communities in the nation; these communities hold practically the entire American nonfarm population.

The grant arrangement does not imply that all cities must spend on each local service just that per-capita sum derived from the regression equations; indeed, too much rigidity in expenditure patterns would defeat the very purpose of the arrangement, which is to increase local choice with respect to public expenditures. The grants should clearly be labeled "general purpose." (In England they are called block grants.) If a given city is efficient enough to spend less than the predicted amount on police services, for instance, then the city should be able to use the money saved to purchase other services as it chooses. At present this kind of choice does not exist in many densely populated cities, for even though a city may be relatively efficient in providing police services, its requirements for public safety may still be much higher, say, in downtown areas than they are in suburban areas; thus "municipal overburden" may make it practically impossible, without this kind of grant, to spend any important sum on parks, libraries, and recreational activities in general.

Two suburbs, one lower middle class and the other upper class, will serve as examples. The former may desire public golf courses, tennis courts, pools, and the like, while the latter may satisfy itself for these services in private ways—on estates and in clubs. The lower middle-class suburb might then use its public funds for the public amenities mentioned, while the richer suburb converts its grant—presumably small in any case—into local tax relief. (We believe this kind of choice should be allowed, too.) The important thing to note, however, is that a better financed and more analytically defined revenue structure is a necessary condition for long-term improvement in the quality of life in urban areas. Presently, grant systems for nonschool services do not recognize special expenditure requirements of densely populated areas. (Revenue sharing has improved the situation slightly but by no means enough.) This can be seen when we compare grants for nonschool purposes made by the federal and state governments to central cities and suburbs. In 1967–68 Buffalo received $65 per capita from combined federal and New York State sources in support of nonschool public programs; Buffalo's suburbs Grand Island, Kenmore, Lackawanna, and Tonawanda received, respectively, $89, $86, $185, and $76. Yet Buffalo's spending needs, as estimated in the Brazer regression model, are considerably greater, in per-capita terms, than those of its suburban districts. The same general situation prevails throughout the metropolitan areas of New York.[11] It has also been documented for such disparate states as Delaware, California, and Michigan.[12] Thus the first requirement for improving life in the cities is a radical revision in the allocation of public resources so as to recognize the special needs of densely populated areas for public services.

Other Financial Measures on the Nonschool Side

In addition to the establishment of a system of block grants for municipal services, certain other changes must be made. For one, the federal government should assume financial responsibility for welfare transfers. Presently, welfare transfers are supported from federal, state, and county resources. Where the central city is at the same time a county—for example, San Francisco—or is comprised of a set of counties—as in New York City—concentrated pockets of poverty place an extremely heavy burden on local tax sources. Local costs can reach staggering proportions even when central city residents share local welfare costs with suburbanites who live within the county but outside the central city. Cities contain most of the indigent population, but when local taxes are levied to provide for their living expenses, the wage-earning population of the cities receives no direct benefit—thus local taxes for welfare operate differently from local taxes levied to pay for services, since the wage-earning population *does* obtain direct benefits from public services provided by its city government. One may favor, as we do, income redistribution; but should choosing to

[11] Brazer et al., "Fiscal Needs and Resources."
[12] Betsy Levin et al., *The High Cost of Education in Cities* (Washington, D.C.: The Urban Institute, 1973), pp. 58–59.

reside in a central city or in the county of such a city entail an extra obligation to help finance this redistribution?

Metropolitan revenue-sharing schemes should be developed to reduce the financial burden facing central cities, especially in regions where commercial and industrial enterprises are moving to the suburbs to escape city taxes. Such a plan was recently proposed for the Minneapolis–St. Paul metropolitan area in an attempt to break down the barriers between central cities and suburbs and between suburbs and surrounding rural areas and to reduce incentives for fiscal zoning. Fiscal zoning refers to the adjustment of zoning ordinances by some communities to attract certain kinds of development and discourage or prohibit other kinds in order to develop a favorable property tax base. Under the proposed plan, none of the existing tax base of a community will be shared. Forty percent of the net growth of commercial-industrial valuation after 1971, however, would be shared among all units of government—cities, villages, townships, school districts, counties or special districts—in the Twin Cities' area. (The constitutionality of this scheme is currently being tested in the Minnesota courts.)

None of the recommendations we have discussed so far in this chapter, though each serves commendable objectives, really achieves a redistribution of income. More positive measures are needed to reach this end: negative income tax, or, similarly, guaranteed family income. State grants to rescue big cities *could* work in the wrong way to redistribute income if the taxes to improve urban life must be paid for by the poor. It does no particular good, for example, to pour additional state money into New York City if the increase in the state budget is raised by sales taxes and other regressive tax measures. The poor families of New York City, including childless families, would therefore have to provide a major share of the financial resources for the revitalization of the city. Policies to ensure that this does not happen include: increased federal revenue sharing (for the federal tax structure is still more progressive than most state tax structures) and a shift of the state's revenue source toward progressive personal income taxation.

Unionization of City Employees

A special problem faced by city governments is the effect of additional resources on unionized municipal employees and the possibility that unions will absorb money that could be spent on the poor. Some people believe that union members who work for the cities will manage to convert all—or practically all—new money flowing into the cities into increased salaries and fringe benefits. If this is true, the money is, in effect, "wasted." The bargaining position of municipal unions is strong. In the private sector, unions do not typically wish to take strong action for fear that the firm with which they are bargaining will go bankrupt; both union and management share a common interest in the survival of the firm, and both know that no outside power is available to bail out the firm if union demands are out-of-line. When unions bargain with cities, however, they may or may not care whether the given city continues as a viable unit of government. In any case, these unions readily assume that the financially hard-pressed city can turn to its state government for help. When labor demands become extreme in the private sector, the employer has residual strength in his ability to relocate his operations, even outside the country if necessary, and to substitute physical capital for labor. Cities, on the other hand, require services that are city-bound; these services are highly labor intensive, and the very lives of people in the cities depend on them, for instance, fire and police services. For extremely large cities, such as New York and Chicago, strikes by transit workers, on the one hand, and refuse collectors, on the other, can make life within the city physically intolerable if not actually dangerous. Ordinarily, poorer households—which generally are not members of city unions—are most affected by city strikes. Lastly, until recent years, city authorities have not matched union representatives in bargaining skill; nor have they always been willing to do the necessary "homework" in preparation for contract negotiation.

Nevertheless, the degree of professionalism in labor-management relations seems to be on the rise on both sides of the bargaining table. New York City, where the problems are most severe, has been able to increase productivity in certain services: police, fire, and refuse removal, for example.

If cities are excessively vulnerable to union demands in contract negotiations, the main economic issues presented by major public service groups could be negotiated statewide. If nothing else, such negotiation would prevent unions from pitting various local authorities against each other in the bargaining process; yet it might reduce the degree to which public salaries in the city exceed those of public servants in most suburbs. But problems could then develop if cities were no longer able to attract high caliber public employees. There is simply no clear answer to the problem of providing cost-effective public services in densely populated areas. One may reasonably assume that some portion of any new financial resources made available to central cities will be absorbed by increases in public employees' salaries and benefits; and this is desirable to keep highly qualified people working in cities. But since city management is neither weak nor ignorant, it is not necessary to assume that all new money will be used for these purposes.

The Transport Network

It is extremely naïve to assume that middle-class suburbs will quickly welcome hordes of low-income neighbors and inversely that all children who now live in the suburbs and wish access to urban facilities, services, and populations will find their parents eager to establish residence in the center of the metropolis. Yet choice of a specific residential location, a choice ordinarily made by the adult members of a household, should not determine access to public and private facilities for *all* members of the household. At present a family's residential location unduly limits the ability of young people to enjoy public services. City children should be able to visit the suburbs on day trips to use playing fields, open spaces, gardens, parks, beaches, and so on. At the same time, suburban children should have easy access to the museums, libraries, ballet studios, and, in general, to the cultural and ethnic variety found in large cities.

When it comes to transport, however, almost all American children are poor. Children who are under driving age and who wish to go from suburb to city or from city to suburb must wait until parents or older friends offer rides—the possible alternative of hitchhiking carries its own special danger. Neither New York nor Los Angeles has an operating metropolitan public transport system by which people can conveniently get back and forth from suburbs to the central city, except during commuter hours. In Los Angeles, public transport, even within city limits is severely inadequate. The mistaken assumption that there is no demand for transport outside of commuting hours forestalls the development of a transportation system that could accommodate young people. Yet a great deal of transport equipment, including school buses, stands idle many hours of the day and night and is rarely used on weekends. Suburban fragmentation has taken place while interurban transport systems have largely fallen into disuse.

Summary Observations

Due to the courts' narrow definition of "wealth," none of the measures discussed in this chapter—the circuit breaker, progressive DPE, income based supplements and achievement-based supplements, general purpose urban grants, or improved metropolitan transport—is required to satisfy the legal principles advanced by *Serrano*. Nevertheless, their inclusion in school finance reform is essential if corrective measures are to operate equitably. Lower-income families are trapped in the public education system. Already saddled with heavy tax burdens to support public education, they cannot possibly afford leaving the public sector to find alternatives in private education. To be sure, private education can be an expensive alternative even for wealthier families, but at least it remains an option for them. For poorer families there is no choice at all. The absence of choice raises another important problem. The proposals discussed in this chapter serve only to protect the poor from onerous financial burdens. They do little to guarantee that poor families will be more likely to get the kind of education they want. Wealthier families possess the economic and political power to assure them that their desires for educational services will be met. They may form exclusive residential communities providing the kind of public schools they want. They may dominate school boards and, therefore, affect the formulation of educational policy. They can afford private schools that provide the type of special attention they seek for their children.

Although the following chapter retains an economic interpretation, it moves away from simple dollar solutions to these problems. Dollars are essential if families are to have adequate purchasing power; but in addition there must be an effective mechanism for putting those dollars to work. Further, there must be a menu of alternatives available if choice is to be more than mere rhetoric. Thus, in Chapter 5 we will examine the educational marketplace and explore methods for improving its operation. In Chapter 6 we will discuss possible additions to the list of educational services available for purchase.

5

THE EDUCATIONAL MARKETPLACE

Economists, at least in capitalist societies, love markets. They rely on markets to solve problems of what to produce, how to produce it, and how to allocate it. When markets work properly, planners do not need to measure the actual satisfaction an individual gains from consuming specific goods or determine an individual's preference for one commodity over another. No one cares or needs to know, for example, whether you derive seventy utils of utility or fifty from going to a movie. It is simply assumed that if you think the price of admission is worth it, you will go; if you do not think the movie is worth the price of admission, you might choose to stay home and watch television instead. More or less simultaneously, your decision and the decisions of others on whether or not to see a movie transmit information to movie producers. On the basis of box-office receipts—that is, demand—they decide whether to include sex, violence, drama, comedy, or famous actors in their films. Under certain conditions producers might even begin to consider whether it is worth making movies at all. There are no legislative commissions on film making; nor is there a computer-run public agency to determine whether films are effectively satisfying the public. If a comparable market existed for education, you might have saved yourself the price of this book. In the film industry the market does it all, so if you open your local paper to the movie guide and all you can find is half a dozen shows about big-city detectives you can at least be reassured that some people enjoy such fare and, with luck, your favorites will eventually find their way onto the screen.

For producing and distributing some commodities, however, the market mechanism is not very effective and sometimes is quite useless. Economists call this group of goods and services public goods. A public good is one that cannot be divided into purchasable units. There are no feasible ways of excluding nonpaying consumers from enjoying the commodity. Furthermore, although everyone benefits from provision of the service, there is no incentive for a single individual to undertake production. Since everyone consumes the commodity in approximately equal amounts once it is produced regardless of whether he has contributed to its costs and without respect, indeed, to how much or how little he or she has contributed, no one will pay for it unless compelled to do so. From this situation arises one of the classic rationales for government intervention and the power of taxation. Government produces the necessary services and taxes everyone to underwrite their costs.

It is customary at this point for some economists to cite national defense or the lighthouse as examples of public goods and then simply to mention that there are many others. In fact, there are not many others, and the phrase "public good," as used here, should not be confused with goods and services that are produced by government. Schools, clinics, buses, and subways have mechanisms (entrance requirements, fees, fares) that exclude some people. Highway tolls may be relatively unknown to some Americans, but they are part of everyday driving in the northeastern megalopolis. National and state parks have discovered the entrance gate as well as the campground fee, and a sunbather does not soak up much sun on the New Jersey shore without a prominently displayed ticket. Despite the growing popularity of such user charges to simulate markets for government-produced goods, some government services remain "free." With the exception of national defense, education is the largest of these services. Since public education is commonly a product assigned to local government, there is, in theory, a market that governs its production and allocation. But as we shall see, this market is quite different from those to which we are accustomed.

The Tiebout Hypothesis

The process of consumer demand and resource allocation in local government is given an economic rationale in the propositions of Charles M. Tiebout.[1] Tiebout was concerned with the problem of measuring demand

[1] Charles M. Tiebout, "A Pure Theory of Local Expenditures," *Journal of Political Economy,* 64 (October 1956): 416–24; "An Economic Theory of Fiscal Decentralization," in National Bureau of Economic Research, *Public Finance: Needs, Sources, and Utilization* (Princeton, N.J.: Princeton University Press, 1961), pp. 79–96.

for public goods in the absence of market mechanisms. To the extent that local services constitute public goods, service divisibility *within* a local jurisdiction is impossible, and markets cannot operate. Tiebout recognized, however, that different kinds of services and different levels of expenditure can and do exist *among* districts. As long as the benefits of these services do not spill over from one district into another, Tiebout believed, a kind of quasi-market is at work. His model suggests that families satisfy their desires for certain kinds and levels of local public service by "voting with their feet," as we mentioned earlier. Shopping among local jurisdictions offering different tax and service packages, the family locates in the district providing the tax-service package that maximizes its net benefit. The result somewhat resembles a market solution. Supply is differentiated by various competing districts, prices are reflected in different tax rates and housing values, and demand is manifested by consumer movement among different local districts.

The Tiebout hypothesis, as it is commonly called, contrasts sharply with the *political view* of local government espoused in *Serrano* thinking. Under the political view it is assumed that local governments respond in the short run to changes in the household tastes of residents already in place. This assumption explains the repeated assertions that "local control must be preserved." In contrast, under Tiebout's probably more realistic view local governments are unable to make any kinds of important short-run changes in the services they provide. Therefore, household demands are satisfied by a family's choice of a residence according to the value it places on current offerings of the various local governments in their metropolitan area. It is essentially the same process by which households, in theory, regulate resource distribution in the private sector. That is, they choose to buy or not to buy goods and services offered by a particular supplier.

Strangely, the Tiebout hypothesis has never received any substantial amount of empirical investigation. Nevertheless, the proliferation of independent suburban communities surrounding central cities suggests that the Tiebout model may be applicable to metropolitan areas. In the San Francisco Bay Area, for example, a family that is relocating may choose from among nine counties and about ninety municipalities. If the family has children of school age, it may choose from among more than a hundred school districts with levels of per pupil expenditure ranging from $750 to $2,490 and school tax rates ranging from $2.65 to $7.18 per $100 of assessed valuation. Many considerations other than educational quality may affect locational decisions. The family that owns one or more cars may choose a community with easy freeway access or avoid communities that levy local taxes to support public transportation. Families with very young children may gravitate toward communities that provide day-care facilities, whereas childless individuals and the elderly may not. Low-income households may try to find municipalities with significant health-care expenditures; those who can afford private medical attention, on the other hand, may not. The large number of local jurisdictions permits households of similar tastes to locate together and therefore tie the tax-expenditure programs best suited to them to a specific geographic area. In this way competition among local services is minimized, and unnecessary duplication of local services is avoided. The program of various public services of a locality is defined not by external bureaucracies but by the local residents who bear the costs and reap the benefits. In short, as the Tiebout model suggests, the community organizes and governs itself and defines its own interests and priorities.

The Tiebout world is attractive, but if it adequately explains public economic activity of families, why does there seem to be such widespread dissatisfaction with local public services? Several explanations are possible. First and least damning to the Tiebout hypothesis is the fact that many local services are supplied at a zero price. Such services as education, city streets, traffic control, police and fire protection are not provided free—but at the moment they are consumed, the user is charged no fee. Therefore, at the time the service is used, the consumer *perceives* a zero price. Economic theory maintains that consumers will demand a service as long as the utility of another unit, that is, the satisfaction derived from adding an opera component to the local public library's record collection, exceeds the cost (that is, the perceived cost) to them. If the price is zero, they will demand the service as long as another unit is worth more than zero. Consequently, they demand many units of the service whose worth is less than actual cost.

Therefore, zero pricing creates an illusion of dissatisfaction. It induces consumers to think that they want more of a commodity only because they do not perceive the actual cost of the additional consumption. (The reader might ask himself if he would dial directory assistance as often as he presently does if he were charged twenty cents for each call.) Although this argument is quite logical, it is probably more applicable to services provided by state and federal governments. Local services are financed primarily by local property taxes. Except in communities dominated by renters, the property tax is highly visible, billed in large annual or semiannual lumps that provide a striking reminder that local services are not free.

Moreover, of all major taxes property taxes are most directly related to the services they finance; many communities indicate this by itemizing the taxpayer's statement and specifying what fraction of the bill is allocated to schools, sewerage, fire protection, and other services. Thus, the prices of local services are quite apparent.

A more likely explanation for dissatisfaction with local services is that Tiebout's market simply does not work, or at least it does not work well for many households. Several problems indicate strongly that the Tiebout model falls short of any optimal market solution. First, the model relies heavily on household mobility. Since the individual household probably cannot effect changes it might prefer in local services (the "you-can't-fight-city-hall" syndrome), its only alternative is to relocate in another community whose services and taxes reflect the family's tastes. But residential location carries with it a rather high degree of permanence. Costs of relocation are high, in the expenditure of money and physical, mental, and emotional energies. In addition, factors other than public services—travel distance to work, family ties, and proximity of friends—may also determine residential location. Further, zoning regulations and racial or ethnic discrimination may block a family's move into the community having the tax-service package it desires. In brief, adjusting residential location to meet changing preferences for local public services is no simple matter.

Another problem occurs if the Tiebout market is to work efficiently. It requires that households having similar tastes be able to locate themselves in homogeneous, geographically bounded jurisdictions. Homogeneity of tastes is essential to the market because the services are financed by a general tax (the property tax) levied at the same rate throughout the jurisdiction. A household desiring fewer services than the amount provided cannot petition to have its tax bill reduced even if it consumes less or none of the services. It might be added that the problem may not be as severe for households desiring more of a certain service if this service has a counterpart in the private sector. Parents can and do, for example, purchase private tutorial services, music lessons, books, and so on, to supplement public education. Privately supplied security personnel are also a rapidly growing method of supplementing public police services.

But to what extent can we achieve geographic homogeneity? Increasingly there are signs that social and political organization in America is becoming more nonterritorial in nature. Greater personal mobility, the exponential growth of information and communications systems, and general technological advancement are contributing to an ever-growing diversity of life styles, occupations, avocations, and interests. While two families may agree on the type and level of educational spending they prefer, they may be adamantly opposed on issues of public legal services, pollution control, low-income housing, street improvement, rapid transit, park location, and so on. As the number of issues increases and society becomes more heterogeneous, geographic homogeneity can be achieved only by extreme geographic fragmentation. The clearest example of geographic fragmentation is the "retirement village," generally existing as a new town of white middle-aged residents sharing a common interest in golf and a common need for security gates and patrols. If fragmentation does not occur (and municipal boundaries are often difficult to change), households inevitably are dissatisfied. But fragmentation itself can lead to dissatisfaction, if only because economies of scale are lost. Thus our present reliance on territorial government does not seem well-suited for the future, and it certainly suggests that if the Tiebout model was once valid, it is quickly becoming obsolete.

Finally, the Tiebout market totally fails to relieve inequities resulting from household income distributions. In all fairness, Tiebout actually never suggested that his model compensates lower income households for their lack of purchasing power in his quasi-market. At best, his market implies that low-income families that are desirous of a high level of local services can locate in communities with large expenditures. But they would have to sacrifice housing services by purchasing cheaper, smaller houses or renting smaller apartments. Federally subsidized low-income housing in our central cities may even make this sacrifice of housing services unnecessary. Few local services are "pure" public goods, however, in the sense that a level of service provided to one household is automatically and necessarily provided to all. Streets may be cleaned and improved in one section of the city and left unattended in another. Experienced teachers may be assigned to one school, and young, inexperienced teachers placed elsewhere. Police may respond more quickly and devote more thorough investigation to calls from one neighborhood than from another. Park location is often the decision of the local planning commission, and precise placement may be determined by the most influential citizen group in the community. Ironically, the Tiebout model may be invalid not because it fails to provide a market for public goods but because so few local public services are actually public goods. Education, police service, street maintenance, parks, hospital location, and safety are on close inspection divisible goods, in the sense that precise distinctions can be made in types and qualities of services offered to different households; thus, their allocation is easily manipulated. There is little rigorous empirical investigation of the actual pattern of distribution of these goods. Yet we suspect that, like the market for the private sector, those households with the purchasing power get the goods; those without it do not.

The Distribution of Educational Goods

Focusing on the distribution of educational services, let us see how this "market," with all of its shortcomings, operates and what pattern of distribution it produces. There are four peculiarities of educational service to be considered first. If a family is to use the public schools it prefers, it must generally establish residence in the district providing these schools. It may not reside in one town and choose freely from among public schools in neighboring towns. This practice was mandated in earlier times by lack of transport facilities for school children and by the high cost of developing such facilities. Now, however, though transport facilities are improved, the convention is maintained. On the other side of the coin, a family may not always choose freely from among schools within its own town. This strengthens the fact that schools within a district tend to be of one type. If the family has no choice because of district attendance zones or busing requirements, it is assured that it will get the kind of schooling it wants only if every school in the district offers what it wants—that is, only if every school is the same.

A second peculiarity of educational service is that it is generally subject to conditions that have a constant cost of production. A class of twenty-five students requires, for instance, one certified teacher. Teachers' salaries represent the major cost item in public education. As a district's enrollment grows, its expenditures increase proportionally and it saves little money. In economic terms a large district cannot instruct one class of students any more cheaply than a small district.

A large district, however, can provide more specialization of labor in teaching than a small district. Thus it can offer a greater variety of educational programs *at no increase in cost per student over smaller districts*. If a goal of schools is to provide a variety of educational options at minimum cost, it pays to be big. This is an important point because, as we shall see, other factors encourage the maintenance of small districts and thus serve to preempt this opportunity.

A third feature of education is that its costs to the individual family are shared at any specific time with other citizens in the district who do not have children in the public schools. Although a family's direct involvement with the schools may last approximately fourteen years (if it has two children born two years apart, each attending a full twelve-year school program), it pays taxes before its children enter the schools and after they leave. Simultaneously, families and individuals who do not have and may never have children pay taxes and therefore share schooling costs at any specific time.

We are aware that the opportunity costs of a teacher's services, that is, the economic value of the teacher's services in his (or her) best alternative occupation, are borne in the present time period and that, generally speaking, it is not possible to shift the real costs of education from one period to the next. Our discussion in the preceding paragraph might be considered as a process of "spreading costs" over time. Assume, for example, that all households have children. Education is paid for exclusively from a tax on households—by means of a property tax on residences. The period from the marriage of spouses until the death of the head of the household is roughly fifty years. The household may have children in school for fourteen years, perhaps, or 28 percent of its lifetime as a single household. Thus it receives direct services for fourteen years and pays school taxes for fifty years. Over the entire fifty-year period it probably meets the full burden of cost imposed by its children on the district (unless it quickly leaves the community after its children are out of school). But during its fourteen years of direct consumption, the household is a net receiver. It could achieve the same kind of evening out—or spreading—of school costs by making bank loans to meet full-cost tuitions if we did not have our present system of public education. In higher education, where the share of costs borne by public authorities is smaller and where foregone income is a more important element of cost, loan finance is a large and rapidly growing method of cost spreading.[2]

In general, the costs of public school may be shared over a large or small geographic area. Most states have a mixed system of school finance, with the state (large area) meeting about half of the school bill and localities (small areas) paying most of the rest. The fourth feature of education, then, is that small geographic areas usually contribute about 50 percent of school costs.

[2] In England, on the other hand, more use is made of fees in the lower grades; sometimes families borrow the money they need to pay school fees. Also, households in England bear less of the cost of university education.

Keeping these four features in mind, let us see how the operation of our educational system, in its present form, inhibits two important kinds of choice: (1) choice of place of residence and (2) choice of content of educational programs.

Choice of Residence

It is easiest to explain the harmful effects of our educational system on residential choice in financial terms. Table 3 shows what happens to a hypothetical rich school district when its population increases by approximately 10 percent. It is assumed that in year 0 the district has 2,000 households and that every other household has one child in public school. School operating costs are $1,000 a year per pupil, and the district, being rich, receives only a flat grant from the state equal to $250 per public school student. It is also assumed that the district receives no money for education from the federal government. All local taxes in the district are raised by a levy on residential property, and each householder, on the average, lives in a home valued at $40,000. The tax rate in year 0, then, is $0.94 per $100 of full value. In Case I the new families bring in an average of one school child per two families and buy a house worth $40,000. In other words, the new residents are just like the old residents in number of school-age children, tastes for housing, means of purchasing housing, and so on. The tax rate stays constant at $0.94 per $100 of full value.

In Case II each new family brings on the average one child to place in school, with conditions otherwise the same. The tax rate rises by 8.5 percent to $1.02. In Case III not only does each family bring one child, but each family is allowed to buy, on the average, a house worth only $20,000. The school tax rate then rises to $1.07—up 13.8 percent from Case I. In Case IV not only does each family bring in one child and manage to find a house worth only $20,000, but each new child, on the average, requires additional educational services costing $500. (That is, the new children require a school program costing $1,500, as compared with the $1,000 program that adequately serves the longer-established residents.) The tax rate then rises to $1.19, up 26.6 percent from Case I. The increase in tax rate, unmatched by any improvement in the quality of educational services, represents an additional burden on long-time residents; it also probably leads to a decline in house value through the process of capitalization, thus leading in turn to a need for further increases in school tax rate.

There are additional factors that may push local tax rates up in this type

Table 3 Hypothetical Illustration of the Effect of Change in Public School Enrollment on District Tax Rate

	Population (in Households)	School Enrollment	Total School Costs	Grants from State Government	Local Share of School Costs	Local School District Tax Base	School Tax Rate	Percentage Change in School Tax Rate
Case I Year 0	2,000	1,000	$1,000,000	$250,000	$ 750,000	$80,000,000	$0.94	–
Year 1	2,200	1,100	1,100,000	275,000	825,000	88,000,000	0.94	0.0
Case II Year 0	2,000	1,000	$1,000,000	$250,000	$ 750,000	$80,000,000	$0.94	–
Year 1	2,200	1,200	1,200,000	300,000	900,000	88,000,000	1.02	+8.5
Case III Year 0	2,000	1,000	$1,000,000	$250,000	$ 750,000	$80,000,000	$0.94	–
Year 1	2,200	1,200	1,200,000	300,000	900,000	84,000,000	1.07	+13.8
Case IV Year 0	2,000	1,000	$1,000,000	$250,000	$ 750,000	$80,000,000	$0.94	–
Year 1	2,200	1,200	1,300,000	300,000	1,000,000	84,000,000	1.19	+26.6

of situation. If the town includes industrial and commercial property in its school tax base, any given increase in school costs will lead to relatively larger tax hikes than if the town had no such property. (The presence of commercial structures may allow a town to "export" some of its school costs, in the sense that citizens who buy the products of the taxed enterprise and who live in other cities and towns contribute to school expenditures in the given district. But we are talking here not about absolute level of tax rate but about its sensitivity to changes in local expenditures.) Also, if the new students require additional school housing, the total school tax rate will rise to reflect the district's need to pay interest and principal on bonded debt. Finally, new residents may cause an increase in per-capita expenditures in nonschool public services, and the total local tax rate would again reflect such a rise.

To hold the tax rate and individual household tax bills constant, at least three critieria must be met: (1) newcomers must have no more school-age children per family than the average of residents, and they must cause no increase in capital outlay; (2) newcomers must purchase houses of value at least equal to the existing town average; and (3) newcomers must possess no general propensity to require special school or nonschool expenditures on their behalf. A community may assure that these three criteria are met by carefully constructing zoning and building regulations. Land may be zoned strictly for single-family houses built on lots of at least one acre. Limits may be placed on the number of bedrooms in new apartments and condominiums. The town may require private construction and maintenance of sidewalks. Many communities prohibit overnight street parking, thereby forcing construction of parking facilities on land that might have been used for housing. Some even prohibit carports, requiring instead construction of a fully enclosed garage. All of these requirements increase the cost of housing, which in turn effectively screens lower-income households from middle- and upper-class areas. Since lower-income households tend to have larger families and children needing specialized school services, these practices also tend—directly and indirectly—to satisfy requirements one and three. *In short, the structure of the educational system produces stratification of communities by income level and, to some extent, by family size and certainly by differential educational requirements of young children.* Thus obstacles to social class integration are deeply rooted in the basic operation of the educational finance system.

This fact reveals the particularly deleterious effect of the fourth feature of education, namely, that costs are shared to a significant degree over *small geographic areas.* If the state government, for example, undertook to pay the costs of running schools and recognized fully the needs of some students for special services, costs would be shared over the geographic area of the whole state. If this were the case, the observations drawn from Table 3 would be totally in error. From a strictly financial point of view, and with respect to the costs imposed on local residents to pay for public schools, it would no longer matter what kinds of families moved into an area. Indeed, the reader might wish to produce examples of his own in the format of Table 3. As the share of state support becomes larger, approaching, say, the 50-percent mark of aid received by the typical district of average wealth in the typical state, the effect of new residents on increasing the school tax rate is moderated from what is shown in our example—but it is still quite noticeable. At 100 percent it vanishes, of course, unless the new children are especially expensive to educate.

Choice of Content of Educational Programs

The existing system of education impedes curricular choice because it maintains incentives to create school districts of small size. Smallness in education has a major drawback. On cost grounds, small school districts, even ones that are well-financed, cannot afford a great degree of specialization of staff or diversity of courses and programs. Small districts cannot establish a Bronx High School of Science or a school for children who are working in theater or musical productions. They are limited further, in the number of foreign languages and the variety of vocational options they can offer.[3] The situation is compounded by frequently moving households. Also, when a middle-class household moves from one small suburb, it is likely to move into another small suburb. If one of the suburban school districts adopts highly innovative programs, it places a handicap on its stu-

[3] One of the authors recalls the dismay his daughter felt when she was unable, because of a crowd, to talk to a visiting harpsichordist after he had given a performance in her junior high school. With great kindness her regular teacher said, "Put your question to me, I'll answer it." The student confided in her parents: "I wanted my question answered by a person who plays the instrument, not by someone who has just read about it." The opportunity to work face-to-face with highly specialized talents in a wide range of fields is necessarily confined to big school districts. They can spread the costs of any particular specialty over a large enough number of students who have some narrowly defined interest. It would take a fair-sized district to produce, say, twenty-five budding scientists who are seriously interested in the archaeology of the Indus Valley; yet, the topic is extremely fascinating to those who do have such an interest.

dents who depart in mid-flight, educationally speaking, for they will have to orient themselves to a less diversified program than the one they had previously. All districts, then, must stay pretty much in line with each other and provide a standard educational program.

Now, we may ask, why does our system of education establish preference among adults to live in—and make use of—small school districts? It is, of course, no accident that there have been as many as 1,400 units of local government within the two counties of Long Island and that 131 of these were school districts. Partly, the reason is financial and stems from the same conditions that produce social class stratification. On fiscal grounds middle- to upper-income communities are overwhelmingly attractive to people who are not affluent themselves. If a poor family can find a cheap house in a rich town, its members enjoy the twin benefits of a low tax rate and expensive public services. The entry of lower-income families into a wealthy town is likely to drive up local tax rates, however. Older residents suffer a dual loss when this happens: they have to pay higher taxes for the same or lower quality public services while at the same time the value of their local real estate falls. The larger the suburb, the higher the absolute number of houses that will turn over in the market in any given year. The larger the number of vacant homes, the greater the probability that some of these homes will find buyers whose incomes are lower than the community average. Thus if the tax base is to be maintained and control of expenditures protected, it is safer to be small.

Another reason the system leads adults to prefer smallness is based on the convention that a child attend school only in the school building designated by district authorities. Reliance on the conventional pattern that parents have no power to choose the school their child will attend actually encourages curricular standardization. Let us take it for granted that in our country middle- and upper-income families choose for the most part to make use of publicly provided schools. Such families will seek to exercise control over the school services their children are to receive. One means of control is to shop among different schools to find the one school that appears to offer the program best suited for each child. If an error in judgment has been made, the family might then remove the child from one school and place him or her in another. This method of control—that is, control through the exercise of choice—is ruled out by (1) the fact that middle- and upper-income families prefer public education and the particular form of cost sharing that such a decision implies and (2) the convention, noted previously, that a child must attend school in his or her district of residence. Control, therefore, must be exercised by maintaining access to the school authorities, namely, the local school board and the superintendent. If such access is truly to yield a measure of control, however, it is important that the school district be small.

Concluding Comments on Present District Structure

The socially stratified pattern of suburban living may provide incentives for families to move up the economic and social ladder. Perhaps an upwardly mobile family needs to know that it has the opportunity to find a safe place in which to live; perhaps it helps to see this safe place in a neighboring community.[4] It does not seem as necessary today, however, for educational opportunities for children of a household to be so closely determined by the decision of the household's adults in picking specific residential location. Consequently, we should turn to possibilities for improving the market mechanism, seeking ways to allow parents to choose from among a greater range of educational programs on behalf of their children and even to afford a degree of choice to students themselves.

Education, as we have mentioned earlier, is the most costly service provided by localities. Under the present finance system its costs are extremely sensitive to family characteristics. Under either FSA or DPE, though, taxpayers would no longer have to be concerned if incoming families had more children than the average resident family or if they chose to live in a house of modest value. Moreover, under a new plan it should be easier to redraw district lines in order to create school districts of proper size. Thus the financial pressure that now serves to keep districts small would largely be deflated. Finally, as districts grew larger, they would be able to offer a greater range of program options to their students.

Yet one financial impediment to social class integration in education would still remain. Low-income students often require extra school services. If this fact is not recognized, an FSA plan would require a receiving district to shift resources from ordinary students to newcomers from low-income families who had educational disadvantages. Under DPE school tax rates would probably rise in such receiving districts as new students

[4] See the testimony of Anthony Downs, *Hearings before the Select Committee on Equal Educational Opportunity of the United States Senate* (Washington, D.C.: Government Printing Office, 1971), pp. 2971–77.

who are expensive to educate move in and localities recognize their unique needs. Both of these unfortunate results could be avoided by establishing appropriate categorical-aid programs for both low-income and low-achieving students, as we discussed in Chapter 4. That is, FSA and DPE are incomplete reform measures, but a more comprehensive set of proposals is readily available.

To increase choice with respect to place of residence and type and range of educational programs is an important objective. It stands quite independently of misplaced concerns that *Serrano* reform would merely raise teachers' salaries and misplaced doubts about the effectiveness of compensatory education grants that may not yield startling short-run gains for students. Such concerns and doubts seem to be the current stock-in-trade of some critics of the *Serrano* decision and the reform effort it has created.[5]

Improving the Market Mechanism

So far, we have seen that the existing system of distributing educational resources is characterized by three basic flaws: (1) it permits distribution of educational resources and tax burdens on the basis of a largely irrelevant criterion—district property wealth; (2) it perpetuates social class segregation; and (3) it limits variety in educational services by encouraging the proliferation of small school districts that cannot afford curriculum specialization. These, then, are the three major problems that any proposed remedy must attack.

Of the many proposals advanced to improve school finance, only one purports to deal simultaneously with all three of these problems. Labeled *family power equalizing* (FPE) by its creator, John E. Coons, this proposal is a sophisticated voucher system.[6] A voucher is simply a piece of paper representing some dollar amount that may be applied to a purchase of a specified commodity. It places dollars (actually cash in kind) directly in the hands of a consumer and enables him to choose the quality and quantity he desires of the commodity (within the limits of his budget—voucher plus any supplement from his own monetary income). An example of a voucher

[5] Chester E. Finn, Sr., and Leslie Lenkowsky, " 'Serrano' vs. the People," *Commentary*, 54, no. 1 (September 1972): 68–72; Daniel P. Moynihan, "Equalizing Education—in Whose Benefit?" *Public Interest*, 29 (Fall 1972): 69–89.

[6] John E. Coons, "Recreating the Family's Role in Education," *Inequality in Education*, Harvard Center for Law and Education, nos. 3 and 4 (1970): 1–5.

system is the Food Stamp Program. The idea of using vouchers to purchase educational services is frequently attributed to the writings of Milton Friedman. [7] The concept has a long history, however, and is mentioned in the writings of John Stuart Mill, Tom Paine, Adam Smith, and several others.

The mechanics of the scheme are best explained by its author:

> Basically, the statute [draft legislation to establish a voucher plan] would create an educational market offering products (schools) at several distinct levels of per pupil cost. Within this market proprietors—public and private (the system could be made exclusively public *or* private)—would compete for the custom of buyers who have been made substantially equal in their power to purchase admission at these various per pupil cost levels. To establish that equality of purchasing power the draft statute conditions access to any school within the system upon an equivalence of economic sacrifice for every family choosing that school, irrespective of family income. Each family's selection from among schools of varying per pupil cost would represent also a choice among varying rates of a special tax to be levied upon the family's income; but the tax burden on families of different incomes choosing schools of the same per pupil cost would, in economic terms, be rendered equivalent by means of a progressive rate structure.
>
> For example, upon enrolling its children in a school costing the minimum of $500 per pupil, a family with an income of $5,000 would become subject to a levy of, say $25 (.5%). Access to a $1,000 school might cost that same family $60 (1.2%). Enrollment in these same schools by children of richer families would create correspondingly greater tax liabilities. Not only would the tax be proportionately larger for wealthier families, the rates would also be adjusted to account for diminishing marginal utility. However, even for the richest family, the tax liability in absolute terms would never exceed twice the per pupil cost of the most expensive class of school permitted in the system.
>
> The family's yearly educational tax liability in absolute terms could range from nearly zero to $3,400. A welfare family choosing the cheapest class of school would pay perhaps $5.00; a very wealthy family choosing the most expensive class would pay the maximum. The total tax would not vary by the size of the family; thus the hypothetical wealthy family with two children attending a school spending $1,700 per pupil would "break even." Concededly, the ceiling on the tax violates the principle that sacrifice must be equal; it is a concession designed to assure that the richest families would not automatically desert the system for purely private schools. The number of such families above the break-even line can be made very small, but there is little to be gained by driving them out of the system for the sheer sake of consistency.

[7] Milton Friedman, "The Role of Government in Education" *Economics and the Public Interest* (New Brunswick, N.J.: Rutgers University Press, 1955).

Schools are classified in two ways: (1) a division is made between schools which are public (Categories "A" through "D") and private (Categories "E" through "H"); (2) all schools, public and private, are divided into four per pupil cost levels each for K–8 grades and high school grades. As currently drafted (much depends upon the wealth of the state) the schools would be permitted to spend the following amounts per pupil:

	A and E Schools	B and F Schools	C and G Schools	D and H Schools
K–8	$500	$ 800	$1,100	$1,400
High School	$800	$1,100	$1,400	$1,700

Public schools in the system would be administered by a state superintendent and board (county and district authorities would cease) with authority to unify or decentralize that administration for some purposes, but with general protections for academic freedom of public school teachers and with a detailed requirement of financial decentralization, as we shall see. Private schools would qualify to enter the system essentially by meeting the minimum standards imposed upon those private schools outside the system that satisfy the truancy laws. Each private school would decide for itself under which of the four statutory levels of cost it would operate; this decision would also fix the rate of the family tax required for attendance at that school. For each public school that choice would be made by the superintendent based largely upon demand in the area for each level of per pupil cost with its accompanying tax. For every school—public and private—the superintendent would maintain a drawing account containing the appropriate number of dollars per student enrolled for schools of that class. The dollars would be earmarked by student and a pro-rated share would move with the student from school to school if he transferred during the year.

The funding of the total system would be based primarily upon statewide sources such as a state income tax. The special family tax described [previously] is designed principally as a vehicle for measuring family interest in education. Clearly it would not fund the bulk of the total cost of the system. This means that the cost of education would be broadly distributed but also that the primary beneficiaries would pay an additional cost representing a rough estimate of the value to them of the purely private benefit.

Because of its commitment to the market mechanism the draft statute financially isolates each school (public and private), limiting its income (with certain exceptions) to the amount fixed per pupil by statute for its class. This is a guarantee of equality in competitive position. If the state were permitted to pour additional money into a public school that was failing to attract students, the market stimulus to excellence would be diluted, and children in the nonfavored schools would be unfairly treated; the same would be true if private charitable sources sought to shore up a failing private school.[8]

Consequently, under FPE a voucher carries two prices. One price is its transactional value in the marketplace; the other is its price to the consumer. Vouchers with the same market value have different purchase prices depending upon the income of the consumer. Clearly a major difficulty in developing voucher systems is this determination of relative purchase prices. If, as the courts imply, educational services are not to vary with varying wealth (income in this case), then purchase prices must be progressive. A household would rationally weigh only the additional cost of moving up from a low-expenditure to a high-expenditure voucher. The additional increments would have to be significant enough for members of a given income class to prevent all members of that class from choosing the most expensive voucher. For a $4,000-a-year family of four, prices for vouchers of $800, $1,100, $1,400, $1,700, and $2,000 might be $150, $250, $350, $450, and $550, respectively. The $400 difference between the cheapest and most expensive voucher would probably discourage most low-income households from picking the most expensive level. To keep prices progressive, absolute prices for similar vouchers would be greater for middle-income households and still greater for high-income households.

Keeping prices progressive effectively places a floor under prices offered to high-income families. Ideally, the relative prices would be such that the perceived prices for a given market value entail the same perceived sacrifice from everyone. The real world, however, actually puts a ceiling on prices to high-income families. The ceiling is related to costs of attending schools that choose not to be recipients of vouchers (assuming there is not an easy way to prevent the wealthy from opting for such schools). This puts a crimp in the system. Even if all households with school-age children are required to choose at least the minimum voucher and pay the corresponding price, a range of more than $3,000 between the least and most expensive vouchers would probably drive wealthy families out of the system. This could happen because the price of public education would be approaching the price of private education. Consequently, the range of prices for the poor cannot be very wide either. This diminishes somewhat the income-equalizing effects of the system. Yet all is not lost, for educa-

---

[8] Coons, "Recreating the Family's Role in Education," Harvard Center for Law and Education, nos. 3 and 4 (1970), pp. 2–3. Reprinted by permission.

tional resources would still be allocated much more in accordance with consumers' preferences than they are under the present system.

One of the major criticisms leveled against the voucher system is that it is an impractical, idealistic scheme that would ruin the present system of financing public schools. Property taxes now produce over 50 percent of school receipts. The property tax cannot be abandoned without creating potentially serious economic distortions. Moreover, recent reexamination of the property tax suggests that it should not be abandoned even if it were possible to do so. The tax appears to be progressive as its effects are more carefully studied.

However, a voucher system need not depend on abandoning the property tax. A modified form could be integrated with the present system, and it would go a long way toward enabling consumers to express their preferences for different educational services. Existing property tax revenues could be translated into a minimum voucher available to all parents for use at the school of their choice. This would be a basic grant available to all consumers at no additional charge. The state could establish this minimum amount, say $750, and finance it by a statewide property tax. State revenues for education from other state taxes could then be used to supplement the user's contribution toward higher-priced vouchers. Consumers could select their voucher at the market value they desired, the actual cost depending on household income and number of dependents. The cost determination could be made when the consumer filed his state income tax. Then payment for the voucher could be included with the tax statement, or if the amount is too large to be made in one payment, payments could be made quarterly to the state's tax board.

The scheme is not as far-fetched as it may appear, and an abbreviated version is currently underway in San José, California. There the Alum Rock School District budget provides a basic voucher for each child—$850 for primary grades and $1075 for grades 7 and 8. No tuition supplements are allowed, and the degree of choice is limited. Parents in the district are allowed to send their children to one of thirteen public schools, whichever they choose. The staffs of the schools have developed a total of forty-five offerings ranging from the traditional structured program to the innovative "School 2000." Each program's budget depends on how many students it attracts. Because the Alum Rock experiment is only in its second year of operation, its effects are difficult to judge. Tom Fay, principal at the Donald J. Meyer Elementary School, reports:

We've filled two classrooms that were empty last year, and we've had to get a mobile classroom on top of that, which shows parents liked what we had to offer.

Unexcused absences are down, vandalism is down, and the kids obviously feel better about school. They have done at least as well as they would have done normally. . . . The teachers have worked far and above what they did before. They're tired, but they're pleased with themselves.[9]

Meanwhile, in New Hampshire a similar program is being considered for September 1974 that will include private and perhaps parochial schools and permit parents to supplement vouchers from personal income sources.

How well do vouchers correct the three major flaws (outlined earlier in this section) in the existing system of distributing educational resources? If the minimum voucher of $750 were financed through a uniform statewide property tax with the protection of a circuit breaker, certainly the nexus between district property wealth and educational spending would be broken. Further, suppose that no tuition supplements from private income were permitted if a family participated in the voucher program. (Although all parents of school-age children might be required to purchase minimum vouchers, presumably they would not be forced to use them. They could seek schools outside those recognized by the voucher system.) Then, voucher supplements with prices progressively determined by family income would also ameliorate the effects of personal wealth in educational spending. Thus it is difficult to find fault with a voucher system on the grounds of fiscal equity. Under a voucher system, however, public costs might rise substantially, especially in states in which large numbers of children now attend private or parochial schools. At present taxes paid by parents of private and parochial school children go almost entirely to support children in the public system. Under a voucher system—provided the courts rule that such indirect financing of parochial education is constitutional—all parents would have a claim on public funds. Whether total spending on education, private and public, would rise and, if so, by how much are questions that are not easily answered. Thus a family might find that although its combined tax costs (from property, income, and sales taxes) are much higher under a voucher system, this figure might not exceed the previous total for the family's tax and private school costs. At present it is certain that poor families would find their total costs reduced, while costs to wealthy families would increase. Moreover, poorer families

---

[9] *The New York Times,* 3 June 1973, "The Week in Review," p. 11.

now using private or parochial schools would probably obtain larger cost reductions than a poor family that is now using the public system. Families presently using the private system contribute to public school costs, but the reverse is not true. In short, FPE would redistribute income vertically from rich to poor and horizontally from public to private.

Would vouchers encourage social class integration? Again, we cannot say with certainty. Vouchers do destroy the *economic* arguments for excluding low-income families from middle- and upper-class suburbs, at least for purposes of education. Since the minimum vouchers are paid for by a uniform tax and voucher supplements are income equalized from general state revenues, educational costs would be spread over the entire state. The local tax base becomes an irrelevant factor in determining educational expenditure. Consequently, excluding low-income families on grounds of protecting the local tax base could no longer be justified. Some communities might attempt to continue exclusion, claiming that the tax base must be maintained for local services other than education. But in most middle- and upper-class communities education represents from 55 to 75 percent of local costs, so that the argument is somewhat weak.

Critics of FPE argue that despite the fiscal equity achieved by a voucher system, vouchers would not ameliorate social class segregation and might even encourage it. They point out that exclusion on economic grounds is merely a guise for deeply rooted racial, ethnic, and social class prejudices that FPE does not attack. They also argue that by allowing parents freer choice of schools, vouchers might well promote racial, ethnic, religious, and social segregation. Moreover, insofar as vouchers introduce competition among schools and therefore require schools to advertise achievement results, vouchers encourage schools to "skim," that is, to select only the best students and thereby promote segregation according to academic ability. Clearly choice per se is not necessarily good or socially helpful. Some controls are necessary, and this need for control produces a dilemma. As controls become more comprehensive and detailed, real diversity in educational offerings diminishes. It is pointless to offer people choice unless diversity exists. Controlling the kinds of faculty private schools may hire, for example, tends to limit alternatives that otherwise might be presented: a school in a mixed neighborhood that had no blacks on its teaching staff might not appeal to black students and a school staffed solely by graduates of denominational teacher training institutions might not appeal to agnostic students, etc.

Drawing the line between necessary and unnecessary controls under a voucher scheme is no simple task. Requiring that strict racial quotas be met in each course offered may prevent a course from being offered at all. Conversely, if no racial requirements are established, the development of white and black separatist schools is possible.

Nevertheless, we can no longer see our existing educational system as the only alternative. Each of the various proposals for change we have considered has strengths as well as weaknesses. In Chapter 6 we will examine a way of combining the best that each has to offer while simultaneously attempting to minimize the risks that each proposal implies.

6

FINANCE REFORM FOR THE
COMING DECADE

Throughout our analysis of school finance, we have maintained that policy reform must be evaluated within a framework of three broad objectives: (1) reduction of fiscal inequity that presently produces allocative patterns closely related to district wealth and family income; (2) amelioration of the racial and social class segregation encouraged by the existing finance system; and (3) expansion of the educational alternatives available to individual households dissatisfied with the uniformity of the public school system. In some detail we have examined three general proposals now being widely considered as potential solutions to the issues raised by the courts and educational reformers.

In our estimation each proposal has its drawbacks, for none meets all the objectives we consider essential. DPE, while eliminating inequities produced by district property wealth, fails to counter the effects of household income unless it is supported by a circuit breaker and income-based grants. It weakens considerably the economic rationale for racial and social segregation, but it offers no guarantee that schools will be more responsive to the desires of parents and students. Under DPE districts would be free to choose levels of expenditure, but the nexus between educational service and household residence is not broken. Families must still express preferences largely through the cumbersome and expensive process of relocating their homes. FSA, like DPE, reduces fiscal inequity and protects opportunities for achieving racial and social integration but only at the risk of severely limiting the availability of educational alternatives. Under FSA

119

the market is reduced to the political forum. Differences in expenditures are possible only on the basis of educational criteria deemed appropriate by legislatures. Thus only those adept at getting the ear of political representatives are able to express their educational preferences. Finally, FPE achieves fiscal equity and provides the most certainty that families could choose the type of educational services they prefer. FPE severs the relationship between household location and educational service. Therefore, it would probably stem the exodus from city to suburb and might even partially reverse this flow. Encouraging educational consumerism, however, could considerably undermine attempts to achieve racial and social balance in the schools. Courts and administrative agencies would be hard pressed to distinguish imbalances motivated primarily by racial discrimination from those motivated by desires for specific educational alternatives.

In short, none of these proposals adequately achieves the results implied by our three objectives. Each provides a large measure of fiscal equity if sufficient attention is paid to the effects of a given plan on the school tax burdens of low-income households. But aside from fiscal equity considerations, choosing one proposal over another requires a trade-off between integration and consumer choice. Most reformers have reluctantly concluded that this trade-off must be made and that a state must choose one variation of the three proposals as the basis for its school finance system. Thus a state that chooses to implement FPE must sacrifice possibilities for achieving integration. Alternatively, the state might implement DPE and protect integration policies, but then it diminishes the prospects for consumer satisfaction. No single state can enjoy both benefits.

We, too, must conclude that furthering integrative policies requires sacrificing freedom of choice and vice versa. We believe, however, that this trade-off should be viewed from a different perspective. There is no inherent reason why a state must choose only one of the three reform measures. It could choose instead to finance different segments of its educational system with different finance plans. It might choose FSA, for example, as the basis for its elementary schools, DPE for its middle schools, and further modify DPE—by adding vouchers and interdistrict choice—for the high school level. Such a decision still implies trade-offs, but it allows priorities to be established for each segment of a state's school system rather than for the system as a whole. Viewed in this light, the three proposals offer a significant opportunity for change, and it is within this framework that we sketch our preferred school finance system. The sketch evolves from a simple outline: FSA at the elementary level, DPE for middle schools and high schools, with voucher supplements and interdistrict mobility at the high school level.

The sections that follow are somewhat different from earlier ones. Rather than merely describe an "ideal" financing scheme, we will try to sketch some of the various educational programs that might be offered in a revised system. We think this outlook is important—to ensure that school systems are humane and effective, finance reform must be accomplished in conjunction with expansion and revision of educational offerings.

In the areas of curriculum and pedagogy, we are not necessarily more expert than the reader. For this reason we will not attempt to catalog all the possible changes that might be envisioned or the variety of teaching styles and methods that might affect a student's education. Perhaps our recommendations will seem idealistic or incomplete to experienced educational practitioners. Yet we think it is vital for people to think about what schools themselves—not merely tax bills and expenditure levels—might look like if financing arrangements were changed.

Elementary Education

Our preference for FSA at the elementary school level is based first on our conviction that at this level integration policies should hold sway over consumerism. We share the view espoused by Walter Shapiro that "one should not be embarrassed about clinging to the still touching 1950s image of black and white children playing together in a schoolyard. It may not exude radical chic and may seem naive in this justifiably cynical age, but it has the rare virtue of being right." [1] Our concern is not limited to racial integration. In an increasingly heterogeneous society children from diverse life styles and varied economic strata should be able to interact with one another. From early exposure to diversity, hopefully they will learn that differences need not be feared and that there is only false security in prejudice. In this vein the Fleischmann Commission noted:

> For most children, the first experience with the legal and political framework of their society is in the school. . . . The best traditions of our country, those of which we are proudest and which we try, in our explicit teaching, to transmit to

---

[1] Walter Shapiro, "Black and White Together Is Still the Point," *The Washington Monthly*, 4 (June 1973): 42.

our children, envisage a heterogeneous, but fraternal society in which individuals are free to identify with and develop their own special cultural heritage if
they choose, but in which no hard lines will be drawn separating group from
group and citizen from citizen. This Commission believes that a school system,
maintained by law, governed by public officials, supported by public revenues,
cannot, by acts of commission and omission, permit the young who come into
its charge to draw the inference that public authority accepts, encourages or
participates in, the division of our society with first- and second-class citizens.[2]

Secondly, we prefer FSA at the elementary level because, although
there may be widespread disagreement about methodology, there exists
some consensus on the general objectives of elementary education. Elementary education lays the foundation for future specialization in school,
career, avocations, and everyday interests. It is thus concerned with "ba-
sics." It seeks to provide every student with elementary competence and
awareness in reading, mathematics, the arts, science, history, personal and
social relationships, and physical and mental health. Equally important, it
seeks to instill (or, perhaps more accurately, preserve) excitement in learning, pleasure in the process of exploration, and joy at the moment of intellectual discovery. It seeks to quell fear of error and the anxiety created by
failure. Elementary school is in large measure society's way of greeting its
young people and introducing them to the world they have inherited.

Yet uniformity of purpose does not imply uniformity in procedure. By
recommending FSA we are by no means recommending mass production
of elementary education, casting each school, each classroom, and each
teacher in the same repetitive mold. Each child is unique in some sense.
Since a classroom approach well-suited for one student may be wholly
ineffective for another, each student should be exposed to an approach that
meets his or her requirements. The degree of diversity such an individualized outlook demands can be achieved within a single school at the elementary level. Open and traditional classrooms, for instance, can certainly
exist within the same school. Capital expenditures are not significantly different for either, and economies of scale are not at issue when the objective
is to accommodate different philosophies or methodologies. A teaching
method should be introduced in an elementary school whenever there is a
large enough group of students to form a class that would benefit from this
method. Thus the crucial ingredient in the elementary grades is a school

[2] *The Fleischmann Report on the Quality, Cost, and Financing of Elementary and Secondary Education in New York State*, vol. 1, (New York: Viking Press, 1973), p. 226.

faculty for whom diversity is challenging and nonthreatening. This is not a simple order but one that we believe is attainable.

Intraschool diversity is also necessary at the elementary level, because transportation under a system of alternative schools could present formidable problems. If the system were to give real choice to lower-income families, transportation would have to be available for their children. Six- and seven-year-old children simply cannot be expected to cope with the confusion of crossing Manhattan via public transport. Transportation provided by the school district would be impractical, since a dozen different children in a given neighborhood could well be going in a dozen different directions. Consequently, since geographically defined school attendance zones are essential, diversity will be possible only if alternatives are available at each assigned school.

At what expenditure level should FSA be established for elementary schools? We cannot say with any precision. We suggest as a minimum the existing state average expenditure per elementary pupil. Districts currently spending above this level would be frozen at their existing per pupil expenditure, and measures to correct the remaining imbalance would be phased-in over several years. (Phasing-in FSA is discussed in Chapter 3.) The new FSA per-pupil expenditure, however, represents only a base level. FSA does *not* imply equal spending on each pupil. On the contrary, it means spending according to justifiable educational criteria. Where special needs can be identified—disadvantages incurred from home and community environment, learning disabilities, physical handicaps, and so on—additional spending is permissible and, we believe, essential. Thus FSA does not eliminate the need for income-based grants or achievement grants. Extra allotments, specifically targeted for children with special needs, would be added to the state funds received by each district.

Middle Schools

As its name implies, middle school is characterized by transition. During middle school years, the student, now an adolescent, makes the physical and emotional changes from child to young adult. Simplistic ways of thinking in terms of black and white, good and evil, begin to yield to abstract grays as the world's complicated values creep into the student's awareness. He or she becomes more conscious of change with all of its uncertainties. It is a time of frequent sorties into the adult world and hasty retreats into the safety of childhood. These contradictory impulses produce numerous tensions and frustrations in students attending middle schools.

It seems incongruous to introduce finance into the discussion of these metamorphic years. Dollars, or more accurately what dollars can buy, seem very far removed from the needs, concerns, and curiosity of middle school students. Perhaps it is this distance between money and educational process that leads us to tread softly and cautiously. Nowhere else in the educational system are we less confident of our ability to suggest how much money is needed or how this money should be spent. We believe that integration still holds priority over choice at this stage, but we are aware that during these middle school years the time is rapidly approaching when integration and desegregation cannot be used synonomously. As students become aware of themselves, physically, mentally, and emotionally, they also become acutely conscious of their differences, real or imagined, biologically or socially ingrained. Childhood prejudices absorbed subconsciously now begin to be expressed openly. If schools are to have any success in coping with the emergence of prejudice, they must maintain racial, social class, and sexual heterogeneity. Consequently, we are reluctant to open wide the doors of choice during the middle school years.

On the other hand, a strong case may be made for program diversity in middle schools. Although instruction in grades 6 (or 7) through 9 must continue to stress basic skills in reading, English composition, mathematics, and science, most students are ready to explore new subject areas and begin making preliminary decisions about their future educational careers. In addition, numerous opportunities are available for implementing district-wide programs in such areas as outdoor education, music and art instruction, theater, elementary computer science, and environmental studies. One district may want to organize a music camp, while another may prefer offering wilderness camping expeditions to its students. Still another might wish to make computer facilities available. A program considered frivolous by one district may be deemed essential by another. We feel strongly that districts should be able to make such judgments relatively free of state interference. If districts are to do so, FSA is an inappropriate mechanism. Clearly, these programs carry different per-student costs, and a state-mandated expenditure level would limit a district's options. Hence, DPE for middle schools provides more flexibility in program development, but it preserves opportunities for promoting and maintaining integration in each district's schools.

High Schools

If truancy, drop-out statistics, and low achievement scores are any indication, it is obvious that the present pattern of high school education is not attractive to a large number of students. In most of our high schools rigidly structured school days, inflexible curriculum requirements, and mindless disciplinary codes deny students independence and decision-making power at the same time that society is pressuring them to act more "adult." It is our firm belief that after consultation with their parents and other advisers, high school students are quite capable of deciding (decisions should not be irrevocable) how best to use their time. Entrance into the adult world should not destroy pleasure in learning, and, obviously, students are more likely to enjoy educational programs they have chosen for themselves.

It is also our suspicion that at the high school level, forced desegregation loses most of its effectiveness. At this time integration is most likely to be achieved through qualitative experiences arising from common interests. Mathematical standards for racial, social, and sexual balance seem ineffective where black and white, rich and poor, male and female can interact within an area of shared excitement and curiosity. Nor are we overly concerned when only three whites in a class of twenty participate in exploring the origins of jazz or when two blacks enroll in a course of thirty whites studying French Impressionism. In short, we believe that the opportunity to participate should be open to all; but at this level of sophisticated and specialized interest *compulsory* participation to achieve desegregation or the failure to offer alternatives that might upset racial or social class balance in a classroom is absurd. The opportunity to use educational resources suited to one's needs and interests overrides to a certain extent the importance of integration quotas.

Therefore, at the high school level we prefer a mixed finance system that incorporates aspects of both DPE and FPE. Above a specified minimum, say $800 per pupil, high school districts would be free to spend any amount they choose and tax themselves according to the DPE schedule established by the state. Students would be free to apply to schools outside their own district of residence if local schools did not offer the alternatives they desired; however, public high schools would give priority to district residents. Additional places would be allotted randomly to students from outside the district. (Random allotment is essential if "skimming"—that is, school segregation along the lines of perceived talent—is to be avoided.) If the program costs of the school were higher than the DPE expenditure level in the student's own district, the student's parents would apply for a voucher to cover the excess cost. The price of the voucher would be determined by the family's income. Suppose, for example, that a student living in a district spending $1,200 per pupil wants to attend a high school in another district offering a special program in computer science. The cost of this program is $1,400 per pupil. The student's parents could apply for a $200 voucher from the state. If the family's income reported in its last tax return was $5,000, the price of the voucher might be $25. (Parental contributions for vouchers of given value would go up as household income increased, though not necessarily in linear relationship. A family with $15,000 income might, for example, be required to pay $125 for a $200 voucher.) The difference ($175) between the value of the voucher ($200) and the price to the household ($25) would be made up by the state government. The remaining $1,200 cost of the program would be transferred from the student's district of residence to the high school the student chooses to attend. If the outside program cost less than the per-pupil expenditure in the district of residence, the district of residence would keep the difference.

In addition to being able to choose schools outside one's own district, a student would also be free to choose among schools within the district of residence. Within districts high schools could be structured in a variety of ways. The Fleischmann Commission recommended two broad categories: continued high schools and vocational schools. *Continued high schools* would probably be the choice of most eleventh- and twelfth-grade students; but this does not mean that high schools should "continue" in the traditional manner. Instead, students should have a variety of schools from among which to choose; for instance, "comprehensive high schools" could offer a variety of programs, including academic and vocationally oriented courses as they now do. Other high schools could be organized around a particular concept or theme and be clearly identifiable by their unique environment or teaching styles. A school might be dedicated, for example, to combining in-school study with community experiences, whereas another might attempt to provide opportunities for independent study. Finally, some schools could be specialized on the basis of subject matter and concentrate on sciences, the humanities, or the arts. Thus choosing to attend a continued high school would be only a preliminary choice. After this decision a student would choose the kind of high school he or she wanted to attend.

The subject of vocational education is quite complex. We will spend some time discussing it for a very important reason. Too often vocational education is thought of as the system's "stepchild," and little attention is given to its improvement. We believe, however, if there is to be *real* choice for high school students, vocational programs must be strengthened. A system that provides choice among only academic alternatives denies choice to a great many students.

In regard to vocational education the Fleischmann Commission noted: "While most schooling is ultimately vocational in the broadest sense, courses designed to prepare students for specific jobs at the end of their high school years have a more immediate burden of relevance than college-preparatory, liberal arts courses." [3] Vocational education is greatly affected by external conditions, especially the shape of the labor market in general and the accuracy of projections about future labor force needs. Even if vocational programs are exciting and imaginative, they must ultimately be judged on whether or not they provide entry into rewarding jobs. Vocational training that does not lead to employment must be considered useless.

Before considering specific proposals concerning vocational education, it is worthwhile to list some external factors that affect vocational training and that must be considered in any program revision: (1) Government must act to reduce unemployment in general and the high rate of youth unemployment in particular. One possible way to reduce youth unemployment would be to develop a program of national youth service. [4] (2) Accurate labor force projections are needed, so that vocational programs can be revised in light of actual employment needs. (3) Too often, students view vocational programs as a dead-end in terms of employment and further education. The successes of graduates of vocational programs must be reported to disprove this stereotype. (4) Cooperation among businesses, unions, and the schools in skills training is necessary to ensure that graduating students find meaningful jobs. (5) Coordination must be developed between secondary vocational programs and academic and technical programs in universities, colleges, and technical schools. In this regard Amer-

---

[3] Ibid., p. 72.
[4] Donald J. Eberly, "A National Service Pilot Project," *Teachers College Record* 73, no. 1 (September 1971): pp. 65–79.

ican educators should look to the example of the English "Further Education System," a set of specialized institutions that provide an educational sequence distinct from the academic high school-university model.

In light of all these external factors, what can be done to improve vocational training in secondary schools? Comprehensive high schools should offer vocational courses for which there is student demand; we cannot foresee the day when there is no student market for typing or automotive-repair courses. More importantly, teachers and counselors in all secondary schools should be able to counsel students in the realities of the labor market, thereby equipping them to make decisions about their educational futures. Vocational courses should also be provided in existing vocational high schools and regional education centers. Finally, public schools should make use of vocational expertise that already exists within the community by developing cooperative ventures with private vocational and technical schools.

The last point, an important one, deserves more careful consideration. At this time, given the high costs of vocational training and the continual need to update machinery and training materials, it seems especially foolish to build up vocational programs in public schools when private schools already have the machinery and materials at hand. Computer hardware and software are very expensive, for example; often they are beyond the financial reach of local school districts, even large ones. Computer-programming institutes now exist in most large cities, however, and have the hardware needed to train students in computer skills. In areas like computer programming and data processing public schools should develop working relationships with private schools. The special nature of private vocational schools would add a welcome degree of professionalism to vocational training. As the Fleischmann Commission noted:

> Unlike public institutions, private vocational schools must attract students by proving they train workers who meet the requirements of prospective employers. Thus, private schools are forced to stay up-to-date and keep abreast of changes in the labor market in order to survive. In addition, training in private vocational schools is closely geared to the time required to learn vocational skills; training is intensive and students are free to begin courses at different times during the school year.[5]

Students could be provided with a state-financed voucher redeemable for instruction in private vocational schools, regulated and monitored by state

[5] *The Fleischmann Report,* volume 2, p. 88.

education departments. In this manner, rather than building up expensive vocational plants in local schools, districts would be using scarce financial resources in the most logical manner. Of course, this voucher system must be carefully regulated by state education officials to ensure that no substandard vocational schools spring up suddenly to capture a corner of the state-financed market and also to ensure that private schools charge no higher tuition to the state than to private parties.

Students who choose to attend private vocational schools for grades 11 and 12 should be encouraged to split their last two years of secondary school between the vocational institutions and the public schools. In this way students would be able to advance in the important areas of reading, mathematics, and English composition as well as gain occupational skills through intensive vocational training.

Early College

Finally, a third general alternative, early college, would be available to students who have reached the end of compulsory school age and are about to enter grades 11 or 12. Early college would be an alternative for any highly motivated student who is able to work in the more independent environment of a college or university. Probably only a small number of students are mature enough to tackle the social and emotional problems of going off to college at age sixteen. Those students who do choose early college would most likely do so after grade 11. Grade 11 would still be spent in a continued high school, especially one that stressed independent study or in-depth concentration on a few subject areas. The Fleischmann Commission envisioned a variety of methods by which a student could enter college before the usual time: (1) admission to a campus of the state university; (2) enrollment at a state university "school without a campus," such as the Empire State University in New York State; (3) admission to a local community college; or (4) admission to a private university. Although this alternative is one that will be chosen only by a small number of students, it is one the educational system should offer to those students who will find secondary education repetitive and boring no matter how thoroughly it is restructured.

Note that nowhere has it been suggested that the "general track," by whatever name it is known in senior high schools, should be maintained. Little teaching or learning goes on in general track classrooms; it is not surprising that most school truants and drop-outs come from these classes. Moreover, too often the general track becomes the dumping ground for those students having behaviorial and learning problems. Once in general classrooms, these students get little special help, and their problems seem to multiply. Sometimes, especially in large cities, minority-group or low-income students are channeled into the general track without regard to their interests or tastes; students whose first language is not English are often left to sink or swim—usually to sink—in general classrooms, instead of being provided instruction that they can understand. If an educational system chooses as its goals to develop competence in basic skills and provide the means to continue education or seek employment, there is no place for an amorphous, unproductive general track.

Education Reform and Teachers

Establishment of the financial reform recommended here, namely, state assumption of costs of elementary education and local determination of junior and senior high school budgets under DPE, creates a problem in the determination of teachers' salaries. At present teachers and school boards negotiate to set up a district-wide schedule for salaries and fringe benefits that applies to all certified teachers at all school levels. (For this reason the pay plan is called a single-salary schedule.) If the state is the agency that sets, even indirectly, the level of elementary salaries, while the locality determines the salaries of junior and senior high school teachers, it would be purely accidental if the single-salary schedule were preserved in any district.

One way to deal with the problem is to indicate before hiring that teachers working at different levels in the system should expect to receive different salaries. An elementary teacher would then be prepared, for example, to receive a smaller monthly check than a high school teacher. Teachers would not, in all probability, find this suggestion acceptable; in fact, they would be likely to see it as a step backward. We are inclined to agree.

A more forward-looking possibility is to establish statewide bargaining for teachers' pay. The single-salary concept could then be preserved. Out of the negotiation process would come a set of regional salary schedules applicable to all teachers within a given region. This method has equity to recommend it. Studies of the education process have shown in rather consistent fashion that the most important school variable affecting students' performance is characteristics of the teacher.[6] As long as rich and educationally minded districts are free to set whatever level of pay they wish, they will bid away the most talented teachers from poorer and slower moving localities. This jeopardizes children in poor districts simply because they are poor—the very result we are trying to avoid.

In addition, statewide bargaining should improve fiscal management. As the Fleischmann Commission noted:

> We are not convinced that small locals of larger teachers' unions make good bargaining partners. Over the years, unions have developed techniques of whipsawing local districts. Thus, local unions try to avoid early agreements, since the prime benefits of whipsawing accrue to those who settle late rather than early. The bargaining process becomes unduly protracted, and this in turn distracts conscientious school board members from giving serious attention to instructional questions.[7]

Other Opportunities for Reform

The finance plan we have outlined in this chapter offers numerous opportunities to make other needed educational changes of a less economic character. Therefore, we turn to six other areas in which reform is suggested: teacher training, early childhood education, programs for the gifted, specialized services and regional authorities, year-round schooling, and school administration.

Teacher Training—the Professional School

If teaching is to be made more effective, schools must give more attention to preservice and in-service training of teachers. To accomplish this objective, the Fleischmann Commission recommended the establishment of Professional Schools "to serve the complementary function of exemplary teaching, teacher training and applied research. Professional schools

---

[6] See, for example, James S. Coleman et al., *Equality of Educational Opportunity* (Washington, D.C.: Government Printing Office, 1966). A similar finding appears in Charles S. Benson, *State and Local Fiscal Relationships in Public Education in California* (Sacramento, Cal.: Senate Fact Finding Committee on Revenue and Taxation, 1965).

[7] *The Fleischmann Report*, vol. 3, p. 214.

would fill a role analogous to that of teaching hospitals in medicine. . . . These schools must be large, each accommodating approximately 3,000 students from kindergarten through Grade 12." [8] How might such schools affect the training and effectiveness of teachers?

Now, the teaching profession is largely undifferentiated. A teacher may move up the salary scale as he or she gains years of experience or amasses credits for completion of postgraduate courses, but there is no job scale according to which a teacher rises. An experienced long-time teacher is often treated in the same way as a novice, except perhaps that he or she may receive a fatter paycheck each week. The state could establish, however, through certification procedures and salary schedules, four categories of teachers with different responsibilities: intern teacher, classroom teacher, special teacher, and master teacher. Intern teachers would be beginners in the profession and would spend two years in a professional school as apprentices to an experienced, successful teacher. After a minimum two-year apprenticeship, an intern teacher could apply for certification as a classroom teacher. In addition, there would be a number of special teachers working throughout the system, including reading and mathematics specialists, teachers of bilingual classes and vocational subjects, and teachers of handicapped children. Finally, master teachers, comprising no more than 10 percent of the teaching force and receiving salaries comparable to that of school principals, would be responsible for training and research as well as for classroom teaching in professional schools.

The plan is attractive for a number of reasons. First, it ensures that the crucial task of teacher training would be carried out by the most competent teachers in the system. It would provide incentives, in the form of higher salaries and prestige, for good teachers to continue teaching instead of being lured away by administrative positions. Second, it would standardize the training that beginning teachers receive and better equip them to face the realities of a classroom after an apprenticeship period. Third, professional schools would upgrade teaching in large cities where it is sorely needed and provide a highly visible focus for research and training activities. In an educational system that is grounded upon superior teaching—a basic requirement of this system is to turn out competent, imaginative students—the preparation of prospective teachers and the continuing education of practicing teachers are vital.

There is another important reason to establish professional schools. At

[8] *The Fleischmann Report,* vol. 3, p. 188.

the present time we know remarkably little about how teaching works or how learning occurs. Though governments spend vast amounts of money on education, no one can make accurate judgments about what changes in resource utilization will achieve desirable changes in educational outputs. There is little consensus about which educational resources—for example, teacher skills, materials of instruction, and so on—should be developed or at what point in a student's educational career these resources should be concentrated.

The basic problem seems to be that our educational system is poorly equipped to learn from itself. The results of applied research in education are seldom cumulative. As professionals, teachers play an unconscionably small role in applied research. Professional schools could help to change this situation. In a professional school teachers would be able to bring the ideas they had garnered from their day-to-day experience in the classroom. If several teachers reported similar findings, a set of properly designed experiments could be run to see if the teachers' observations possessed generality. As centers of applied research, staffed with both clinical and theoretical specialists, professional schools could make education more scientific. In this way education might develop as medicine has; professional schools would be analogous to the teaching hospitals that greatly improved the training of physicians, nurses, and technicians and provided, at the same time, centers for medical research.

Although professional schools do not currently exist in the United States, they have been established in the Soviet Union. The Moskvoretskii District Department of Education has organized its schools into groups of ten to twenty and designated one school in each group as a demonstration school. Here faculty from other schools in the group may observe the latest developments in teaching methodology, curriculum organization, and educational technology. In addition, the district designates exceptional teachers as senior teachers, who are on call and available to every school in the district to provide assistance in Russian language, mathematics, and other academic subjects. Within each school the district also identifies master teachers. Each master teacher works with from three to six other teachers and holds consultations, visits their classrooms, and organizes study groups.[9] Few school systems in the world have made such an effort to improve educational effectiveness.

[9] Herbert C. Rudman, *The School and State in the U.S.S.R.* (New York: Macmillan Co., 1967), pp. 177–182.

Vouchers for Early Childhood Education

Educators in the United States and Europe have lately expressed great interest in introducing children to educational processes before the traditional age at which they enter kindergarten. Early childhood education has two general objectives: to increase the enjoyment of childhood by bringing young children into contact with others, both children and adults, from outside their immediate family circles, and to help prepare children for their subsequent entrance into more formal educational programs. By 1973 three states—Florida, Hawaii, and Massachusetts—had passed legislation creating an office of child development (or its equivalent). The Hawaiian act requires a subcommittee of the Governor's Commission on Children and Youth to "develop a statewide, community-based program to meet children's needs," and to "assist children and their parents or guardians in obtaining the assistance and services which the child needs and which are provided by state and local agencies."

Though the objectives of early childhood education seem clear enough, there is little agreement about such matters as which agency is to supply the services, the type of services to be supplied (educational, health, nutritional, supervisory), the methods of child care to be employed, the extent to which programs should emphasize clinical diagnosis and prognosis, and so on. It is not even certain which children can benefit from early exposure to education; some children may, indeed, be better off at home.

To foster creativity in this area and allow parents full choice about whether or not to enroll a child in a given program, states should establish voucher schemes for early childhood education. As in the case of interdistrict vouchers for high school students, parental contributions should be scaled by income. Moreover, both public and private institutions should be eligible to obtain funds from the state through the voucher mechanism.

Gifted and Talented Students

One group of students needing special attention in a newly humanized school system is exceptionally gifted and talented students. Many people think that exceptionally bright students have no difficulty in school; they simply work at their own pace and excell. But too often these children grow bored and dissatisfied with the usual school program and perform well below their abilities. A national report—The Marland Report, published in 1971—stressed this irony: the gifted are the most handicapped group in the schools when their mental age is compared with the age level at which they are taught.[10]

Even more troubling is the fact that those gifted students who are identified and given special programs are overwhelmingly from middle- and upper middle-class families. This really is not surprising, since school districts that can afford to provide enriched programs are usually wealthy ones and, therefore, are populated with wealthy families. Less wealthy school districts must apply limited financial resources to the basic subjects and cannot usually support "enrichment programs." Thus, in another way, we see that reliance on local district wealth to finance educational offerings leads to inequities in educational provision; the poor continue to get poorer. To counteract this situation, the Fleischmann Commission recommended a novel program:

> [T]he state should identify the 200 elementary schools in the state with the greatest concentration of children whose families are eligible for Aid to Families with Dependent Children (AFDC). Using guidelines to be established . . . each such school should undertake to identify the most gifted and talented 5 per cent of its 6- to 10-year-old enrollment. We propose that such children receive special instruction within the school itself for periods of time, not to exceed 10 per cent of the school year. During such instruction the children would be encouraged, under sensitive supervision, to embark on projects together, in small groups or individually, the purpose being to stimulate their interests in exploiting their exceptional characteristics.[11]

In many cases the programs could be coordinated by the staff in professional schools. Whenever possible, "enriched" courses in art or computer science, for example could also be provided after school hours or during weekends. A set of regional enrichment centers throughout a state, filled with scientific laboratories, a well-stocked library, music practice rooms, art studios, and outdoor grounds on which to test agricultural methods and learn how things grow would be an improvement for any educational system. Frequent exchanges between city students and those in the country would add a great deal also.

In the long run a successful program for gifted and talented children need not be completely separated from the normal school program. Mathe-

[10] "Education of the Gifted and Talented" (Washington, D.C.: Government Printing Office, August, 1971).
[11] *The Fleischmann Report,* vol. 2, p. 51.

maticians, scientists, artists, writers, and musicians, for example, could spend time in schools, consulting with all classroom teachers and devoting extra time to working closely and individually with gifted students. Also, all students should become aware of the cultural and intellectual resources of their communities; museums, art galleries, and concert halls should not be reserved only for cursory field trips. It is a saddening fact that city students and teachers must often ignore the wealth of opportunities around them and concentrate on overcoming the problems of poverty, racism, and miseducation in their schools; rural and suburban students, for their part, might have more time for enrichment yet really have nowhere to go within their own communities. A truly successful and equalizing school system would strive to give city children strength in the basic education so that they can benefit from the extras around them and, at the same time, broaden the horizons of rural and suburban children who might be ignorant of the style and pace of city life. In this way a school system would truly be training its children for life in the world.

Specialized Services and Regional Authorities

In most states a "middle tier" of educational administration stands between the state department of education and the local districts. Sometimes the administrative unit is the county; in some cases, ad hoc bodies, such as the Boards of Cooperative Educational Services in New York, are involved at this level. Commonly, the regional authorities provide services that are too costly for small districts to handle on their own, for example, programs for the severely handicapped, specialized vocational education, data processing, and research.

An expanded instructional role for regional authorities would allow students to choose from a variety of educational offerings, not restricted to vocational fields, to serve their specialized interests. In many parts of the country students do not have access to any large school district. This is true even of students who live in densely populated areas such as Long Island, New York. Though we hope that small districts will consolidate, that district lines will, generally, become less important in determining access to educational opportunities, and that public transport systems will be improved to allow young people to travel over wider areas, we recognize that such changes will occur slowly at best.

Fully funded by the state, regional authorities could supplement the instructional role of local districts, based on demand. Each authority might produce a spring catalog of courses to be given in the following academic year—or in the summer—if enough students signed up to justify the costs of providing the course. Such a program would allow students to explore fields not included in the standard curriculum and to work more intensively—or at a more advanced level—in other fields. Neither of these opportunities could be readily provided by a local district.

The Continuous Learning Year

The continuous learning year, or year-round school calendar, appears to be an idea that is taking hold. Its economic advantages in particular make it attractive. As the cost of building and managing schools rises, innovations that promise financial savings are looked upon in an especially favorable light. A year-round school system can result in financial savings by reducing debt and operational costs through better use of school space and by avoiding new construction, which would no longer be needed if fewer children were attending school at any one time. Because new facilities would not have to be built, school districts could save on both capital outlay and debt service. In addition, the costs of operation and maintenance of new facilities (staff salaries, insurance, utilities) would be saved. Local districts would be able to close obsolete facilities or perhaps convert standard classrooms to other educational uses. Moreover, property normally used for school space would remain on district tax rolls and generate revenue for the locality.

However intriguing these economic incentives must sound to resource-hungry localities, we believe that the educational advantages of the continuous learning year are more compelling than the economic advantages. Under the present pattern of school organization, summer vacation is a period of forgetting, and the first few weeks of fall are a time for review and reteaching. This is obviously a waste of valuable educational time, time better spent on working with problem learners or allowing advanced students to work independently and accelerate. A continuous learning year would bring a measure of continuity to public education; at the same time it would allow for true individualization of instruction. Teachers could work closely with individual students and expect that learning gains would not disappear over a two- or three-month hiatus.

As attractive as the continuous learning year sounds, both educationally and economically, it must be supported by teachers, students, and parents in order to work. In fact, one of the major roadblocks to school-calendar reform in earlier years was popular sentiment that summer is a time for family vacations (even though few parents have two months of uninterrupted vacation to spend with their children). Nevertheless, as school districts throughout the country are experimenting with these school-calendar reforms, people are discovering the advantages of scattered vacations—resorts are less crowded and travel less expensive in the off-season. Moreover, in cases where siblings have different vacation schedules (districts attempt to avoid this, but sometimes it may happen or even be desirable), parents have discovered the merits of concentrating time and energy on one child at a time.

At this point we are not recommending that all states adopt a year-round school calendar; however, we do believe that current laws prohibiting experimentation with varied school calendars serve no useful purpose and should be repealed. Instead, states should pass legislation to allow and perhaps encourage such experimentation. This outlook would allow school districts to revise school-time arrangements in accordance with local tastes and choices, an outcome we heartily approve and one that is in keeping with the other recommendations of this book.

School Administration

Rather than go too deeply into the complexities of school administration, we suggest two changes that would improve the responsiveness of schools to the demands of parents: increasing the responsibilities of school principals and establishing Parent Advisory Councils (PACs). Although principals are very important members of a school community right now, their potential importance is even greater. In fact, a principal should have a major voice in selecting school staff and setting the educational tone of the school. He or she should work closely with teachers, paraprofessional aides, and other school staff to make certain that the ideals of the school are carried out.

Moreover, the principal should work closely with PACs, which would be formed to foster and facilitate citizen involvement in education. Parent advisers should be elected by the parents and legal guardians of a school's enrolled students. Local citizens who are interested in the schools of their area but who do not actually have children enrolled in these schools should have the opportunity to fill positions on the local district school board. But we believe that the PAC should be composed solely of parents. The council should be relatively autonomous and free to express the views of its members on school issues. The PAC should be able to participate with the district school board and superintendent in the choice of the school principal. If the PAC is involved in the selection process, it is likely that its members will work more closely and successfully with the principal once he is chosen. Such a spirit of cooperation between parents and school personnel (both administrators and teachers) is vital for the successful operation and management of a local school. The process of establishing an advisory council and clearly outlining its functions and responsibilities might be time-consuming and complicated, but we believe it would be time well-spent in any school.

Some Concluding Observations

Educational systems serve several different functions. One is to help people prepare themselves to enter occupations and, once employed, to learn the actual, final requirements of the job, whether as architect, bricklayer, medical doctor, or hospital orderly. In spite of occasional economic difficulties, the American economy is extraordinarily productive. Our school system, it is generally agreed, has helped to build this economy.

A second major function of an educational system is to help people develop attitudes that maintain the order and stability of our political life. A cynic might put it this way: "Schools exist to convince us that what we get is what we deserve." Put more positively, schools attempt to inculcate respect for democratic processes and property rights; they help people to determine the boundary between the force of majority rule and the abstract rights of minorities. Outside of some of our major cities—or parts of these cities—we believe that our schools succeed in helping to achieve political socialization.

A third function, important but difficult to describe accurately, is what we may call the development of social consciousness. This is a more active set of attitudes than the set that includes, say, respect for property rights. It is revealed as people try to understand and, indeed, honor the attitudes of others and as they demonstrate the capacity to care for persons outside their immediate families.

The distribution of talent in society is notably uneven. Since we cannot imagine that our educational system will act to suppress talent deliberately, we recognize that institutions of higher and lower education together will continue to widen the opportunity gap between society's more and less talented. The ultimate test of the fairness of an educational system, then, is not found in the question of who pays how much and who gets how much service; the ultimate test is in the question of whether the talent uncovered and nurtured by the system is used to serve or exploit the less advantaged members of society. Hence, we are terribly concerned that our educational system actively seeks to develop a high degree of social consciousness in our young people.

Presently, we fear that our schools are failing to inculcate a sense of social consciousness in students; one explanation for this failure is that the structure of the system itself is not designed with a high regard for the rights of the young, unless one contends, of course, that the rights of the young to choose classmates, to find the educational programs that fit their aptitudes and interests, and to participate in programs in the public sector are properly determined by their parents' choices about where to live and how much property tax to pay. "In effect, the quality of schooling is up for sale. This has long been true for private schools, but from this perspective, the difference between a 'prestige' community with a highly desirable school system is minimal if it exists at all. Home prices are high because the school system is good, or *vice versa.*" [12] Middle-class youth attends school often in splendid isolation from its poorer compatriots, knowing little of the feelings, attitudes, strengths and life styles of the people of poverty. Young people in central cities also attend schools in isolation (in crowded, unserviced neighborhoods) in that they are restricted in knowledge of and appreciation for the values of persons outside their group. Both groups, in too many cases, are denied the intellectual excitement that develops through constant interchange among people of diverse interests, talents, and backgrounds.

Education reform properly deals with disparities in provision of service, and we have spent a considerable time discussing these disparities. We have sought to show, however, that there are other important questions at issue—questions about where people may live and how public-sector programs (in which we are all increasingly involved) can serve a greater variety of individual tastes. As these proposed changes are made, the

---

[12] John E. Tropman and Roger Lind, "Urban Policy Perspectives in the U.S.A.: An Extension of the Yarmolinsky Option," *Policy Sciences,* 4 (June 1973): 224.

public education system will grow to regard with more respect the rights of its primary clients, students, without deference to the status of their parents. In this way the capacity of the system to develop social consciousness should then be enhanced.

The Politics of Change

It may seem that our recommendations for school finance reform are made in something of a political vacuum. We do recognize, though, that changing how money is raised and distributed for educational purposes is not simply a technical problem; the uncertainties and vagaries of the political process certainly play a large part in any reform effort. We acknowledge that our proposals will not be easy to implement. Education is a huge enterprise, one that eats up a great deal of taxpayers' money and employs a large number of people. Thus existing interest groups—school administrators, teachers, noninstructional personnel—might quickly organize in response to new plans that would change the accepted order of things. Many teachers and administrators also recognize that school reform is necessary, but they are likely to feel threatened by proposals that could lower their salaries or fringe benefits or make their job position less secure.

Moreover, we cannot expect the more affluent—who hold a disproportionate share of the political power in this country—to champion the finance reforms we have advocated in this book. First, wealthy people are not being short-changed by existing arrangements; schools in wealthy districts are usually well-equipped and effective. Second, those rich people who are not happy with public schools have, for the most part, the means to send their children to private institutions. Thus their dissatisfaction is shown not by supporting proposals to reform public schools but by withdrawing from the public school system altogether.

We also do not expect either of the major political parties to make school finance reform a plank in its national or state platform. In truth finance reform is not a subject that easily lends itself to partisan politics. Moreover, state legislatures are notoriously unsympathetic to the problems of large urban areas. Although population has shifted to the cities, legislative power remains with representatives from suburban and rural areas. Therefore, state legislators will probably be unenthusiastic about reforms directed toward improving the position of big-city residents, many of whom are poor and lacking in political power. Ample evidence of the ten-sion between state legislatures and big cities is provided by the school decentralization controversy in New York City during 1968 and 1969.[13]

Political success in educational reform demands the development of a new coalition of educational consumers—poor families, civil-service employees, and blue-collar whites who are relatively disadvantaged under existing finance arrangements. These people could join with others who want more effective local government to push for needed reform. Such a coalition could add an element of public-sector consumerism to the process of reform. This kind of consumer action should not be considered far-fetched. The much publicized private-sector consumer efforts of Ralph Nader and others are relatively recent, and yet these, too, seemed impossible a few years ago. The language of local government reform may repel or attract, according to one's taste, but ideas of fairness are easy to grasp and explain. Those who are abused by the present system should at least know the extent of the abuse so they may be better able to enact just and humane reforms.

[13] Richard K. Scher, "Decentralization and the New York State Legislature," *Urban Review* 4 (September 1969): pp. 13–19.

EPILOGUE

Since this book was first conceived, many states have moved toward equalizing the financial ability of local districts to operate schools. We now present a synopsis of some of the legislative changes enacted in the past few months. We hope that other states will overcome their inertia and channel political pressure to pass meaningful reform.

Kansas, in response to a court mandate, passed a bill, during the 1972–73 legislative session, that provides for a variable foundation program. Districts can choose any expenditure level relative to the norm per-pupil budget of $728 (for large districts), but with a minimum of $600. This expenditure level is guaranteed when the district levies local taxes in the same relation to 1.5 percent of local property *and* income wealth as the district expenditure is to the norm expenditure. The local revenue is then raised by property taxes (minus a relatively small income tax rebate). Districts comprising less than 5 percent of the state's enrollment will receive less state aid than previously. This plan differs from DPE in that a district wealthy enough to raise more money than the formula mandates is allowed to keep its money rather than have it "recaptured" for use by poorer districts.

All school finance reform has not been as successful as in Kansas. In a 1973 election the voters of Oregon defeated a constitutional amendment that would have shifted the state's method of financing schools to a uniform state assumption scheme. All districts that spend below $900 per student would have been allowed to increase their spending to $900 while those spending above this figure would not be able to raise expenditures more than 6 percent. Districts would be required to levy a uniform two-mill school property tax rate (a one mill tax rate is a one-tenth of one percent tax rate) and would have had no further control over spending. This loss of local control over spending, fear of greater state control over program content, and uncertainty about the effect of a massive tax shift from property taxes to ability-to-pay taxes (personal income, corporate income, and business profits) led to the defeat of the measure. If education could be divorced from taxation, reform would probably be much easier.

On the brighter side, the Florida legislature passed a bill during the 1972–73 session providing a remarkable amount of equalization. All districts must pay a seven-mill levy on assessed value (95 percent of full value) and receive identical amounts for similar students, adjusted for a county-by-county cost-of-living index. (In Florida the school districts are contiguous with the counties.) Different students—those at three grade levels (K–3, 4–10, 11–12) and others who fall into fifteen classifications of handicaps or six kinds of vocational trainees—receive different amounts. An additional three mills may be levied and is partially wealth equalized. That is, districts are guaranteed 7 percent (or 8 percent in 1973–74 and thereafter) of the base student cost for each of these three mills levied. Excess revenues are not recaptured. In addition, categorical programs are provided for transportation costs, capital outlay, meals for needy pupils, bilingual programs, textbooks, and several other programs.

In March 1973 Montana passed a bill in which the foundation requires a *uniform* $4 tax rate per $100 of assessed value. (Unfortunately, assessment practices are not uniform in Montana, but plans are being made to improve this situation.) Excess local revenues are recaptured. An additional levy of $1.50 is wealth equalized so that an amount equal to 25 percent of the foundation level is guaranteed, but excess revenues from this levy are not recaptured.

Utah, already a leader in equalizing educational resources, passed a bill similar to Montana's. The Utah plan provides the foundation amount for a uniform tax of $2.80 per $100 of assessed value (recapturing excess revenues) and further guarantees a minimum yield of $40 per (weighted) student for another $1 tax levied. Students are weighted so that the foundation and supplemental amounts vary according to need. Weights have been determined for school size (that is, extra money for small schools), handicapped students, vocational students, and the costs of professional staffs and administrative services. Utah did not equalize capital costs but did increase state aid for local construction. Also, the Utah bill uses the average of enrollment and average daily attendance in its state-aid formula so that districts with high truancy rates are not overly penalized (since a teacher must be paid whether all children are present or not). But there is still an incentive for the district to keep up attendance.

While North Dakota did not institute a wealth-equalizing plan, it did increase the foundation level to the point where the state's share of the total cost of education will increase from 42 to 70 percent.

Many other states are also redesigning their school finance formulas. But rather than report in detail what each of the states is doing, we urge you to inquire at your own state department of education and legislature.

The preceding examples of reform show that changes are possible. While none of the new plans is fully wealth equalized for all levels of expenditure, we are encouraged by these attempts to increase the ability of poor districts to provide a quality education for their children.[1]

[1] For further comments on recent developments, see Norton Grubb, "Public School Finance in the Post-*Serrano* World," *The Harvard Civil Rights-Civil Liberties Law Review,* 8 (May 1973), 550–570.

INDEX